LET'S MEET THE SUPERFUUD

THE WHOLE 80 HEALTHY, DELICIOUS AND NUTRITIOUS RECIPES

Family Approved Recipes

Lose Weight without Dieting,

Low Cholesterol, Low Fat,

Healthy Protein,

Recipes for Beginners

ROUMIANKA LAZAROVA

LET'S MEET THE BUCKWHEAT - SUPERFOOD

The Whole 80 Healthy, Delicious and Nutritious Recipes

Lose Weight without Dieting, Low Cholesterol, Low Fat, Healthy Protein, Recipes for Beginners

Copyrights

ISBN: 9798550390153

Imprint: Independently published

CONTENTS

Soups recipes *71*

This page intentionally left blank

INTRODUCTION

The healthy foods are already in our kitchen. They are surprisingly affordable and encouragingly easy to cook. No doubt, one of them is the buckwheat.

If you have not heard of buckwheat or have not yet tasted it, then it is time to get acquainted with one of the most useful foods known to mankind.

Many people think that buckwheat is a grain crop. In fact, this is not true. The truth is that buckwheat is a seed related to sorrel, knotweed, and rhubarb.

The buckwheat belongs to a group of foods commonly referred to as superfoods (pseudo cereals) because "culinary use is the same as cereals" due to the composition of complex carbohydrates.

Today, buckwheat is famous mainly for its beneficial effects, including dietary food for weight loss.

Buckwheat is gluten-free!

You can enjoy cooking with buckwheat if you include

these healthy, easy, and tasty 80 recipes for breakfast, salads, soups, main dishes, desserts, and bread. In each recipe, there is buckwheat as a grain or flour. In this book, you will find a wide variety of recipes: gluten-free recipes, vegan recipes, vegetarian recipes, recipes with different types of meat, low-fat recipes, recipes with vegetable fats, and more. Maybe each of you will find a recipe that will satisfy your preferences. The variety of recipes is achieved by combining buckwheat with other ingredients and spices. I like to prepare and consume food, which uses a minimum of ingredients to achieve maximum flavour.

Each of us occasionally likes to make a little detour and make "cleanse the body".

This book provides good easy recipes that can really give you some exciting ideas.

If you use at least once a week the recipes from this book, you will probably find a favourite recipe to your taste. This will be great for your healthy eating.

With these recipes, I balance for a diverse and healthy diet, which gives me enough energy for the whole day. Portions are tailored to the need of my body when I have an average daily load.

1. What to cook with buckwheat

First, we need to choose buckwheat of high quality

- When choosing a grain of buckwheat, I prefer raw, which is pale yellow. The buckwheat of darker colour or reddish tint has usually undergone some processing. If possible, buy whole grains that are ready to be cooked.

- If buckwheat flour is used, it should be stored in the refrigerator or freezer. It is good to use it in memory for a short time, as it naturally contains oils, making you sick faster.

The buckwheat can be ground in a high-melting mixer to make your buckwheat flour.

Buckwheat is an excellent substitute for rice, oats, wheat, barley, pasta, couscous, and more.

2. Handy Hints

- I recommend rinsing the buckwheat for a couple of minutes in cold water.

- The preparation of buckwheat for consumption can be done in different methods, depending on the preferences of everyone.

- When you have bought a package of buckwheat and cook it for the first time, try the boiled buckwheat flavor. It may be slightly bitter. In such a case, it is best after cooking thoroughly to wash the buckwheat with cold water and only then can use it for consumption.

- ***WITHOUT COOKING:*** half a cup of raw buckwheat pour 1 ½ cups of cold water. Allow standing overnight. The next day drains the water. Buckwheat can be used for breakfast, as an additive for salads, soups, and food.

- ***COOKING 3 - 5 MINUTES:*** Buckwheat is not washed prior to cooking. Mix one cup of raw buckwheat with 3 cups of cold water and boil for 3 - 4 minutes.

- You can cook buckwheat in a large quantity. For example, pour 1-cup buckwheat into 3-cup cold water. Put on fire and left for 3 minutes to boil. Then drain it well out of the water. Store it in the refrigerator for 2 - 3 days. So you will have buckwheat ready to be added to soups and dishes.

- Rinse the buckwheat (1 cup) with cold water. Put it in a deep pot. Pour with 2.5 cups of cold water. Cover the pot with a lid. When the liquid boils, simmer for 4 minutes on low heat without opening the pot. Remove the pot from the fire, cover it with a cloth, and leave it for 20 minutes to absorb all the water. The prepared buckwheat can be used for several days. Keep it in a refrigerator.

There are no strict rules and restrictions on the preparation of buckwheat dishes. Use everything that suits your taste and preferences.

3. The Book

This book presents: 80 varied, easy, and delicious recipes for a healthy life. They are great and easy to follow. In each recipe, buckwheat is combined with various quality products: nuts, seeds, fruits, fresh vegetables, meat, chicken, fish, cheese, milk, herbs, spices, etc. are added to the buckwheat.

Buckwheat Breakfast Recipes (9): Buckwheat Pancakes, Gluten-Free; Buckwheat with Butter and Cheese; Buckwheat Pancakes, Smoked Salmon and Cherry Tomatoes; Buckwheat with Dates, Walnuts, and Seeds; Muffins with Cheese and more.

Delicious Snacks Time Surprises (6): Buckwheat Snack Bars, Gluten Free; Butter Biscuits with Cacao; Crispy Crackers with Seeds and more

Salads Recipes (17): Fresh Vegetable Salad with Buckwheat; Iceberg with Buckwheat and Pomegranate; Spinach with Buckwheat and Bacon; Buckwheat Mango Salad;

Buckwheat with Prawns; Buckwheat with Chicken Fillet and more

Soups Recipes (13): Pumpkin Cream Soup and Buckwheat; Red Lentils and Buckwheat; Lamb Meatball Soup; Turkey Breast Soup with Mushrooms; Fish Soup with Buckwheat Noodles

Main Dishes Recipes (26): Salmon Buckwheat Patties; Buckwheat and Portabella Mushrooms Casserole; Buckwheat with Broccoli and Cream; Buckwheat with Sweet Peas, Stuffed Eggplant with Buckwheat and Chickpeas; Vegan Buckwheat Patties; Buckwheat Potato Burger with Cheddar Cheese; Buckwheat Meatballs with Beef and Sauce; Pork Roll and Buckwheat Sauce and more

Dessert Recipes (5): Buckwheat Dark Chocolate Brownie; Easy Buckwheat Tart with Coconut Oil

Bread and Buns Recipes (4): Buckwheat & Chickpea Bread; Buckwheat Buns

4. Benefits of Eating Buckwheat

Gluten-free! It does not contain chemicals.

A source of healthy protein. Buckwheat is an excellent source of plant protein. It can be a meat substitute.

Improves digestion.

It **balances the metabolism** and helps the body get rid of substances taken with other foods that cause health problems.

The buckwheat helps **fight cell aging, reducing the high cholesterol, lowering blood pressure**. It prevents the **cardiovascular system**. It is especially useful **for skin, nails, and hair.**

The buckwheat has a **beneficial effect on people with impaired peristalsis.**

5. For whom it is useful Buckwheat

Buckwheat is suitable for a healthy lifestyle!

If we include buckwheat in your diet, giving the body light and easily digestible, low carbohydrate content, rich in amino acids and vitamins, micronutrients, and fibre. This product is useful for many people, and it is a chance to reduce health problems.

"The Queen of Weight Loss"

The nutritional properties of buckwheat favour the regulation of body weight. The inclusion of delicious buckwheat in our diet is essential because it is a useful tool to lose weight. That is why the buckwheat is often called the queen of weight loss.

For Babies, Children, and Adults

Buckwheat foods give cells a high iron content in any form. Iron needs at different ages can be met with a proper healthy diet. Both babies and adults need iron. It is no coincidence that recently, it is recommended to introduce buckwheat flour in the baby's menu. This is due to the iron, which is especially important for hemoglobin.

Vegans and Vegetarians

Eating buckwheat satisfies without burdening with fats and toxins. Protein hunger is satisfied, which allows limiting the intake of meat and some types of milk, cheese, cream, and others.

Diabetes

The menu of a person with diabetes must include buckwheat in a different form. The low carbohydrate content undoubtedly makes it suitable for people with this type of health problems

High Blood Pressure

When buckwheat is included in the menu, people with hypertension balance the cholesterol levels in their blood, allowing reasonable control of blood pressure and preventing heart attacks and strokes.

High Cholesterol

Buckwheat maintains low cholesterol levels.

Gastritis

By eating buckwheat in any form (seeds, cereals, supplements with buckwheat flour) the body, will receive:

- Easily digestible proteins;

- Non-irritating fibre;

- Trace elements - including iron;

- Vitamins - along with vitamin E, which is essential for the gastric mucosa

This page intentionally left blank

Breakfast Recipes

R. Lazarova

This page intentionally left blank

1. Buckwheat Pancakes, Gluten Free

(gluten-free recipe)

Servings: 4

Ingredients:

- 1 ½ cups buckwheat flour

- 1 teaspoon baking powder (without gluten)

- vanilla to taste

- a pinch of salt

- 1 teaspoon of brown sugar

- 1 ½ cups of low-fat milk

- 2 eggs

- Butter for smear

Instructions:

Mix in a deep bowl the flour, baking powder, salt, sugar, and vanilla. Stir well. Then add the milk and the whipped eggs to them. Heat a pan for pancakes. Smear with butter and pour some of the mixtures. After 1 – 2 minutes, turn the pancake. When it is baked, put it in a warm dish. You can make pancakes (fluffy) or thin crepes. Serve the pancakes with maple syrup and fruit or with cheese.

2. Buckwheat Pancakes, Smoked Salmon and Cherry Tomatoes

(gluten-free recipe)

Servings: 4

Ingredients:

- ½ cup buckwheat flour

- ½ cup gluten-free flour

- 1½ teaspoons dry yeast

- 1 teaspoon brown sugar

- Pinch sea salt

- 1 cup whole milk

- 2 eggs

- 2 tablespoons sunflower oil

- 0.75 oz (20 g) butter

- **Garnish:** 6 oz (170 g) smoked salmon slices, 8 cherry tomatoes - halves

Instructions:

In a deep glass bowl, warm the milk. Add the sugar and yeast. Cover with a kitchen towel and leave for 5 minutes. Then add the oil and flour mixed with the salt, mix well. Cover the bowl with a towel. Allow the dough to stand at room temperature for 1 hour.

Whipping the eggs in a separate bowl. Add them to the dough and mix well.

Heat a non - stick pan and grease with a little butter. Carefully put a mixture for a pancake. Cook for about 2 - 3 minutes on each side until golden brown.

Garnish the pancakes with smoked salmon and cherry tomatoes.

3. Muffins with Cheese

(gluten-free recipe)

Servings: 4

Ingredients:

- 1 egg

- 2 egg white

- 2.5 oz (70 g) buckwheat flour + 1 teaspoon baking powder (without gluten)

- 3.5 oz (100 g) cottage cheese

- 1.5 oz (42 g) Mozzarella cheese, shredded

- 1 oz (28 g) Cheddar cheese, shredded

- 4 – 5 tablespoon whole milk

- a pinch sea salt

Instructions:

In a deep glass bowl whipping the egg and egg whites with a pinch of salt. Add the milk, flour, and cheese. Stir well. Put the mixture in muffin moulds. Fill them up to 2/3 of their volume.

Preheat the oven to 392 F / 200 C. Put the muffins to bake until golden.

4. Buckwheat with Maple Syrup

(vegan, gluten-free recipe)

Servings: 1

Ingredients:

- 3 full tablespoons boiled buckwheat

- grated bark of ½ lemon

- 1 tablespoon of crushed walnuts

- 1 tablespoon flax seeds

- a pinch of cinnamon

- maple syrup or honey to taste (optional)

Instructions:

Put the flax seeds, walnuts, and cinnamon in a deep bowl. Pour them with hot water, cover them with plastic food wrap. Let to stand for 1 - 2 hours or overnight. In the morning, add buckwheat, lemon peel, and maple syrup (honey). Stir and heat in the microwave oven for 40 seconds (at will).

5. Buckwheat Flakes with Chia and Yogurt

(gluten-free recipe)

Servings: 1

Ingredients:

- 4 tablespoon raw buckwheat flakes

- 9 oz (250 g) Greek-style natural yogurt

- 1 tablespoon chia

- 1 tablespoon ground flaxseed

- 1 teaspoon honey

- a pinch of cinnamon

Instructions:

Mix in a glass bowl all the ingredients and stir well. Cover with plastic food wrap. Leave to stand for 1 - 2 hours or overnight. Add pieces of fresh fruit: peach, banana, strawberry, etc. (at will).

6. Buckwheat with Sunflower Seeds and Strawberries

(vegan, gluten-free recipe)

Servings: 1

Ingredients:

- 3 tablespoons boiled buckwheat

- 1 tablespoon of sunflower seeds

- 1 tablespoon ground flax seed

- ½ tablespoon of crushed almonds

- a pinch of cinnamon

- 3 - 4 well-ripened strawberries

Instructions:

Mix in a bowl the sunflower seeds, flaxseed, almonds, and a pinch of cinnamon. Pour over them with hot water. (best in the evening before the breakfast). Then add the cooked buckwheat. Stir carefully. Add chopped strawberries or other fruits according to the season. Serve in a bowl.

7. Buckwheat with Butter and Cheese

(gluten-free recipe)

Servings: 1

Ingredients:

- ½ cup boiled buckwheat

- ½ teaspoon butter

- 2 tablespoons grated Cheddar cheese

Instructions:

Mix in a bowl the buckwheat and butter. Heat them in the microwave oven for 40 seconds. Add the cheese, stir gently. Serve breakfast with a cup of herbal tea.

8. Buckwheat with Dates, Walnuts, and Seeds (vegan, gluten-free recipe)

Servings: 1

Ingredients:

- 4 full tablespoons boiled buckwheat

- 3 dates

- 2 tablespoons of raw cashew

- 1 tablespoon of raw pumpkin seeds

- 1 tablespoon ground flaxseed

- a pinch of cinnamon

Instructions:

Mix in a deep bowl the dates (without the stones), walnuts, pumpkin seeds, flaxseed, and cinnamon. Pour over with hot water to cover them. Leave to stand for 1 hour or overnight. Then add the buckwheat. Stir well. Warm mixture in the microwave oven for 40 seconds (at will).

9. Buckwheat Flakes with Yogurt

(gluten-free recipe)

Servings: 1

Ingredients:

- 4 tablespoons buckwheat flakes

- 1 ½ cups Greek-style natural yogurt

- ½ cup berries, fresh or frozen

- 1 tablespoon ground flaxseed

- 1 tablespoon crushed walnuts

- a pinch of cinnamon

Instructions:

In a deep glass bowl, mix all ingredients. Stir well. Leave to stand for 1 – 2 hours. Then add fruit and serve the breakfast.

Snacks Time Recipes

R. Lazarova

This page intentionally left blank

10. Buckwheat Bars with Dark Chocolate

(Vegan, gluten-free recipe)

Servings: 20 bars

Ingredients:

- 1 ½ cup - boiled buckwheat
- 2.5 oz (70 g) - crushed raw almonds
- 1.8 oz (50 g) - crushed raw hazelnuts
- 3 oz (85 g) - minced flaxseeds
- 1.8 oz (50 g) - minced sesame seeds
- 1.8 oz (50 g) - raw pumpkin seeds
- 3 oz (85 g) dark chocolate chips
- 1 – 2 tablespoon coconut oil
- 3 oz (85 g) dried cranberries
- ½ teaspoon cinnamon

Instructions:

Preheat the oven to 355 F / 180 C. Line a cookie sheet with parchment paper.

Put the dried cranberries in a bowl of hot water. Let them stay for 30 minutes. Then drain the water and add the blueberries to the mixture for the bars.

In a deep bowl, put the buckwheat, all seeds, all nuts, coconut oil, cranberries, and cinnamon. Stir the mixture very well and gently knead until it forms a dough. Lay it out on the cookie sheet. (Select the size of the cookie sheet depending on whether you want the bars to be thicker or thinner). Push it firmly with your palms or spatula and smooth it. Bake it in the oven for 30 minutes. Then remove it from the oven. Turn the mixture over a large board, and let it cool. Cut into 20 equal-sized bars. It is suitable for each bar to weigh not more than 1.5 oz (45 g). Wrap each bar in plastic food wrap.

11. Buckwheat Snack Bars, Gluten Free

(vegan, gluten-free recipe)

Servings: 24 bars

Ingredients:

- 1 ½ cup - boiled buckwheat

- 2.5 oz (70 g) - raw almonds

- 2.5 oz (70 g) - crushed raw hazelnuts

- 3 oz (85 g) - minced flaxseeds

- 1 tablespoon sesame tahini

- 1.8 oz (50 g) - raw sunflower seeds

- 2 teaspoon finely grated ginger root

- 20 dried dates

- ½ teaspoon cinnamon, vanilla to taste

Instructions:

Preheat the oven to 355 F / 180 C. Line a cookie sheet with parchment paper.

Remove the pits from the dates. Pour over with ½ cup hot water for 30 minutes. Then place it in a food processor or strong mixer until it forms a smooth paste.

In a deep bowl, put flax seeds, sunflower seeds, all nuts, sesame tahini, buckwheat, ginger, cinnamon, vanilla, and the pureed dates. Stir the mixture very well. Pour the mixture into the cookie sheet tray. (Select the size of the cookie sheet depending on whether you want the bars to be thicker or thinner). Push it firmly with your palms or spatula and smooth it.

Bake the mixture for 30 minutes. Then remove it from the oven. Turn the mixture over a large board, and let it cool. Cut into 24 equal-sized bars. It is suitable for each bar to weigh not more than 1.5 oz (45 g). Wrap each bar in plastic food wrap.

12. Buckwheat Biscuits

(gluten-free recipe)

Servings: the number of biscuits depends on their size

Ingredients:

- 2 cups buckwheat flour

- 2 eggs

- 3 tablespoons 100 % pure coconut oil, milted

- 10 dried dates

- 1 teaspoon baking powder

- a pinch of salt

- vanilla to taste

- Rice flour (the amount is determined by how much it is necessary to thicken the mixture)

Instructions:

Remove the pits from the dates. Pour over with ½ cup hot water. After 30 minutes, puree them in a blender.

Preheat the oven to 350 F / 175 C and line a cookie sheet with parchment paper.

In a large bowl, mix the buckwheat flour, 2 - 3 tablespoons rice flour, and baking powder. Add the cold coconut oil. Use your fingers to work it in a bit.

In a glass bowl, beat eggs and salt, then quickly add into the mixture. Then add the dates and vanilla.

Mix well all ingredients. When the mixture is just coming together, scrape it out onto the counter and flatten it to ¾ inch thick. Cut out biscuits of the desired shape and size. Put them on a baking sheet and bake for 11 - 13 minutes (depending on size) or until the edges are golden brown. Let the cookies cool on racks before you pick them up.

13. Buckwheat Crispy Crackers with Seeds

(gluten-free recipe)

Servings: *The number of biscuits depends on their size*

Ingredients:

- 4.6 oz (130 g) buckwheat flour

- 4.6 oz (130 g) rice flour

- 4.6 oz (130 g) chickpeas flour

- 2 eggs

- 100 ml - 3.3 fl. oz (US) olive oil or sunflower oil

- 1 teaspoon of salt

- ½ cups of seeds of your choice - sesame, flax seeds, sunflower, pumpkin seeds, poppy seeds, about 200 ml - 6.6 fl oz (US) water

- **Spices:** of your choice – oregano, thyme, marjoram, turmeric, basil

Instructions:

Mix the three types of flour and knead well.

Put the eggs in a deep bowl and add the salt. Whip them well. Add the olive oil, water, spices, and mixture of the three types of flour. You can add ½ of the seeds or keep the whole quantity for sprinkling.

Cover the mixture with a transparent foil. Put it in the refrigerator for one hour. Prepare a suitable tray. Put baking paper and grease it with some olive oil. Divide the dough evenly. Sprinkle with the other seeds. If the seeds do not adhere well on the surface of the crackers, smear with a whipped egg before you put them in the oven.

Preheat the oven to 375 F / 190 C. Put the crackers in the oven, bake for 20 - 30 minutes. Remove the tray from the oven and let crackers cool. Break them into small pieces.

14. Buckwheat Butter Biscuits with Cacao

Servings: The number of biscuits depends on their size

Ingredients:

- 3oz (85 g) - ¾ cup buckwheat flour

- 5.6 oz (160 g) - 1 ¼ cup - whole wheat flour

- a pinch salt

- 1 tablespoon organic cacao nibs

- 4 oz (115 g) butter

- 3 oz (85 g) brown sugar

- 1 egg

- vanilla to taste

- ½ tablespoon powdered sugar, for sprinkling (optional)

Instructions:

Preheat the oven to 355 F / 180 C. Line a cookie sheet with parchment paper.

Sift together the buckwheat flour, whole-wheat flour,

salt, and cacao in a deep bowl. Set aside.

In another bowl, beat the butter and sugar until smooth and creamy. Then add the egg. Transfer the mixture to the bowl with the flour, add, and the vanilla.

Stir in the flour and gently knead until it forms a dough. Refrigerate it for 30 minutes.

Then make out biscuits of the desired shape and size. Lay them out on the cookie sheet. Bake in the oven for 12 – 14 minutes, or until the edges are golden brown. Let the cookies cool before you serve them.

Sprinkle the biscuits with powdered sugar (at will).

15. Buckwheat Granola

(vegan, gluten-free recipe)

Ingredients:

- 9 oz (255 g) buckwheat flakes

- 3.5 oz (100 g) raw almonds

- 3.5 oz (100 g) raw walnuts, cut into pieces

- 1.5 oz (45 g) raw sunflower seeds

- 3 oz (85 g) dried apricots, cut into pieces

- 1.5 oz (45 g) raisins, seedless

- 2 oz (57 g) coconut flakes

- 3.5 oz (100 g) coconut oil

- 4 tablespoons honey or maple syrup

- ½ teaspoon ground cinnamon, a pinch salt, vanilla to taste

Instructions:

Preheat the oven to 355 F / 180 C with a fan. Line a baking tray with parchment paper.

In a small bowl, combine coconut oil, honey or maple syrup, salt, cinnamon, and vanilla.

In another bowl, mix buckwheat flakes, raw nuts, and sunflower seeds. Add the coconut oil mixture to them, mix well until you get a sticky, crumbly mixture. Pour granola mixture onto the parchment paper, in one layer, and bake for about 15 minutes or until golden.

Remove baking tray from the oven, add the coconut flakes, dried apricots и raisins. Stir the granola well. Remove the baking tray from the oven, add the desiccated coconut, apricots, and raisins. Stir the granola well. Leave to cool completely. Then store in a glass jar with a lid.

Serve 3 – 4 tablespoons granola with yogurt, milk, or hot water.

Serve 3 – 4 tablespoon granola with yogurt, milk, or pour the granola with hot water.

Salad Recipes

R. Lazarova

This page intentionally left blank

16. Fresh Vegetable Salad with Buckwheat

(vegan, gluten-free recipe)

Servings: 4

Ingredients:

- 1 cup cooked buckwheat

- 8 cherry tomatoes, cut into halves

- 1 English cucumber, cut into rings

- 2 green onion, chopped

- 3 – 4 sweet mini (baby) peppers, cut into rings

- 1 medium ripe avocado - peeled, pitted, and cubed

- **Spices:** 2 tablespoons finely chopped fresh leaf parsley, 1 tablespoon finely chopped dill, 10 fresh leaf basil, 2 tablespoons olive oil, salt to taste

Instructions:

In a deep bowl, combine all vegetables, avocado, and buckwheat. Season with the spices. Stir gently and serve the salad immediately.

17. Tabbouleh Salad with Buckwheat

(vegan, gluten-free recipe)

Servings: 4

Ingredients:

- ½ cup raw buckwheat

- 1 red onion, finely chopped

- 1 red bell pepper, diced

- 2 beefsteak tomato, diced

- **Garnish:** 8 – 12 green olives

- **Spices:** 10 tablespoons finely chopped parsley, 2 – 3 sprigs finely chopped fresh mint

- **Dressing:** 3 tablespoons olive oil, juice of ½ lemon, a pinch of salt

Instructions:

Put in a saucepan 1.5 cups of cold water. Add salt and the buckwheat. Allow boiling for 5 minutes. Then remove and rinse thoroughly with cold water. Drain it into a colander.

Let's Meet the Buckwheat - Superfood

Mix in a large glass bowl the buckwheat, onion, bell pepper, tomato, and spices. Prepare the dressing and season the salad with it. You can decorate it with a few olives.

18. Buckwheat with Roasted Peppers and Cucumber (vegan, gluten-free recipe)

Servings: 4

Ingredients:

- 1 roasted red bell pepper

- 1 roasted green bell pepper

- 1 roasted yellow bell pepper

- 1 English cucumber

- 4 tablespoons of uncooked buckwheat

- **Spices:** 2 tablespoons of olive oil, 2 tablespoons finely chopped parsley, a pinch of salt

Instructions:

Put in a saucepan 1 cup of cold water. Add salt and the buckwheat. Allow boiling for 5 minutes. Then remove and rinse thoroughly with cold water. Drain it into a colander.

Cut the peppers and clear their seeds. Cut them into small cubes. Cut the cucumber into small cubes.

Mix in a deep bowl the chopped vegetables, the boiled

buckwheat, and the spices. Stir them gently. Serve the salad right after preparation.

19. Buckwheat, Tomato with Parmesan

(gluten-free recipe)

Servings: 4

Ingredients:

- 4 tomatoes on the Vine

- 4 tablespoons uncooked buckwheat

- 4 tablespoons shredded Parmesan cheese

- **Spices:** 1 clove garlic - grated, 2 tablespoons olive oil, 12 fresh basil leaves

Instructions:

Cut the tomatoes into small cubes.

Put in a saucepan 1 cup of cold water. Add salt and the buckwheat. Allow boiling for 5 minutes. Then remove and rinse thoroughly with cold water. Drain it into a colander.

Mix tomatoes and buckwheat. Season them with olive oil and garlic. Mix the salad gently. Sprinkle each serving with Parmesan cheese and basil. Serve the salad.

20. Mediterranean Salad with Buckwheat

(vegan, gluten-free recipe)

Servings: 4

Ingredients:

- 1 cup buckwheat

- 2/3 cup cooked chickpeas

- 1 small red onion, chopped

- 2 handfuls fresh washed spinach leaves – ready to cook

- 2 carrots, cut into thin strips

- 1 tablespoon cilantro, finely chopped

- decoration: 4 lemon slices

- **Dressing:** 3 tablespoons olive oil, juice of ½ lemon, ground black pepper, ½ teaspoon cumin powder, sea salt to taste

Instructions:

First, prepare the dressing. Mix in a small bowl all the ingredients, stir until a homogeneous mixture.

Put in a saucepan 1 cup of cold water. Add salt and the buckwheat. Allow boiling for 5 minutes. Then remove and rinse thoroughly with cold water. Drain it into a colander.

In a large glass bowl, mix all salad ingredients. Add the dressing, stir, and serve with the lemon slices.

21. Buckwheat, Avocado with Cilantro

(vegan, gluten-free recipe)

Servings: 4

Ingredients:

- 4 tablespoons of uncooked buckwheat

- 2 avocado ripe - peeled, pitted, and cubed

- 1 beefsteak tomato, diced

- 2 sprigs of fresh cilantro, finely chopped

- **Spices:** a pinch of salt, 3 - 4 tablespoons lemon juice

Instructions:

Put in a saucepan 1 cup of cold water. Add the buckwheat. Allow boiling for 5 minutes. Then remove and rinse thoroughly with cold water. Drain it into a colander.

Place the buckwheat, avocado, tomato, and cilantro in a deep bowl. Mix them well. Season the salad with lemon juice and salt. Serve the salad immediately.

22. Iceberg with Buckwheat and Pomegranate (vegan, gluten-free recipe)

Servings: 4

Ingredients:

- 1 Iceberg lettuce

- 1 English cucumber, cut into rings

- 2/3 cup boiled buckwheat

- 4 tablespoons pomegranate seeds

- 4 green onion, chopped

- 1/3 cup toasted walnuts, chopped

- **Spices:** 2 tablespoons olive oil, 1 – 2 tablespoons apple cider vinegar, 1/3 teaspoon sea salt

Instructions:

Wash the Iceberg lettuce and then tear to pieces. Mix in a large bowl cucumber, green onion, Iceberg lettuce, and buckwheat. Season with spices. Sprinkle with pomegranate seeds and chopped walnuts. Serve the salad immediately.

23. Spinach with Buckwheat and Bacon

(gluten-free recipe)

Servings: 4

Ingredients:

- 6 oz (170 g) fresh spinach leaves, washed and ready to eat

- 2/3 cup boiled buckwheat

- 4 pieces thinly sliced smoked bacon, diced

- 4 radishes, cut into rings

- 2 green onions, chopped

- **Dressing:** 3 tablespoons olive oil, 1 tablespoon balsamic vinegar, 1 teaspoon Dijon mustard, 1 teaspoon honey, sea salt to taste

Instructions:

Mix the ingredients for the dressing in a small bowl. Stir vigorously.

Mix the spinach, onions, radishes, bacon, and buckwheat in a large glass bowl. Add the dressing, stir, and serve.

24. *Greek Salad with Buckwheat*

(gluten-free recipe)

Servings: 4

Ingredients:

- ¾ cup boiled buckwheat

- 1 English cucumber, diced

- 1 small red onion, finely chopped

- 5 - 6 cherry tomatoes, cut into halves

- 1 red bell pepper, diced

- 1 yellow bell pepper, diced

- ½ cup crumbled Feta cheese

- 1/3 cup sliced green olives

- **Spices:** a pinch of oregano, 2 tablespoons chopped dill

- **Dressing:** a pinch ground black pepper, juice of ½ lemon, 3 - 4 tablespoons olive oil

Instructions:

Mix the ingredients for the dressing in a small bowl. Stir vigorously.

Mix the vegetables, buckwheat, and Feta cheese in a large glass bowl. Sprinkle with dill and oregano. Garnish with olives. Season with the dressing. Transfer salad to a serving platter.

25. Buckwheat Mango Salad

(vegan, gluten-free recipe)

Servings: 4

Ingredients:

- ¾ cup boiled buckwheat

- 1 cup fresh mango chunks

- 1 butterhead lettuce

- 1 cup butter beans in water (cans), rinsed and drained

- 1 beefsteak tomato, diced

- 2 green onion, finely chopped

- 1 medium ripe avocado - peeled, pitted, and cubed

- 2 tablespoons finely chopped parsley

- 1 tablespoon finely chopped fresh cilantro

- **Dressing:** juice of 1 lemon, 3 tablespoons olive oil, ground black pepper, and salt to taste

Instructions:

Wash the salad and then tear to pieces.

Combine butterhead lettuce, boiled buckwheat, mango, drained butter beans, tomato, onion, avocado, parsley, and cilantro in a large glass bowl. Stir thoroughly.

Dressing: whisk lemon juice, olive oil, black pepper and salt to taste in a small bowl.

Pour the dressing over salad and stir.

26. Buckwheat with Prawns

(gluten-free recipe)

Servings: 4

Ingredients:

- ½ cup buckwheat

- 12 oz (340 g) frozen large raw prawns, thawed and drained, ready to cook

- 1 – 2 tablespoons olive oil for fry

- 1 loose-leaf lettuce,

- 1 beefsteak tomato, diced

- 10 pitted green olives

- 1 tablespoon finely chopped parsley, grated zest of 1 lime

- **Dressing:** 3 tablespoons olive oil, juice of ½ lime, 2 cloves of minced garlic, ground black pepper, 1 teaspoon anchovy paste, or 4 anchovy fillet

Instructions:

Put in a saucepan 1 ½ cup of cold water, a pinch of salt, and the buckwheat and bring to the boil. Cover and simmer for 5 minutes on low heat. Then remove and rinse thoroughly with cold water and drained.

Dressing: Combine olive oil, lime juice, ground black pepper, garlic, anchovy paste. Stir well, cover, and refrigerate for 10 minutes.

Wash lettuce leaves and dry them. Put several of them on the serving plate. Cut the remaining leaves into thin strips. To them, add tomatoes, olives, parsley, zest of lime, and buckwheat. Mix well and set aside.

Set pan over medium-high heat. Add the olive oil and the prawns; cook 1.5 - 2 minutes on each side. For each serving: Place ¼ of buckwheat mixture, season with dressing, top with the prawns.

27. Buckwheat Salad with Salmon

(gluten-free recipe)

Servings: 4

Ingredients:

- 2/3 cup raw buckwheat

- 7 oz (200 g) fresh skinless Atlantic salmon fillet

- 6 cherry tomatoes, halved

- 1 each, Hass medium ripe & ready avocado - peeled, pitted, and cubed

- 2 green onions, chopped

- 4 slices of lemon

- **Spices:** 1 - 2 tablespoons olive oil, juice of ½ lime, grated zest of 1 lime, sea salt to taste

Instructions:

Put in a saucepan 2 cups of cold water. Add salt and the buckwheat. Allow boiling for 5 minutes. Then remove and rinse thoroughly with cold water. Drain it into a colander.

Meanwhile, cook the salmon. Heat a non-stick pan to medium-high heat. Once it is hot, add 1-tablespoon olive oil.

Put the salmon and cook for 4 - 5 minutes on each side. Set aside.

Put the buckwheat, avocado, tomato, and onion in a deep bowl. Add with spices and toss gently to mix.

Cut the salmon into small pieces add them in the bowl. Serve the salad immediately with slices of lemon.

28. Buckwheat and Seafood

(gluten-free recipe)

Servings: 4

Ingredients:

- 2/3 cup raw buckwheat

- 12 oz (340 g) frozen raw mixed seafood, thawed and drained, ready to cook

- 1 – 2 tablespoons olive oil for fry

- 1 fresh carrot, thinly sliced

- 1 English cucumber, diced

- ¼ fennel bulb, thinly sliced

- 1 small red onion, thinly sliced

- 1 tablespoon non - pareil capers

- 1 tablespoon finely chopped fresh dill

- **Dressing:** 3 tablespoons olive oil, juice of ½ lemon, 2 cloves of minced garlic, ground black pepper to taste

Instructions:

Put in a saucepan 2 cup of cold water, a pinch of salt, and the buckwheat and bring to the boil. Cover and simmer for 5 minutes on low heat. Then remove and rinse thoroughly with cold water and drained.

Meanwhile, make the dressing. Put olive oil, lemon juice, garlic, and black pepper to taste in a small bowl. Whisk together until thoroughly mixed. Heat olive oil in a large frying pan over medium-high heat. Once it is hot, add seafood and cook for 3 minutes. Mix the buckwheat, carrot, cucumber, fennel, and capers in a deep glass bowl. Drizzle over the dressing and toss gently to mix. Add the hot seafood and finely chopped fresh dill.

29. Buckwheat with Chicken Fillet

(gluten-free recipe)

Servings: 4

Ingredients:

2/3 cup raw buckwheat

- 10.5 oz (300 g) fresh chicken breast fillet

- 1 – 2 tablespoons olive oil

- 10.5 oz (300 g) fresh mix salad greens

- 1small red onion, thinly sliced

- 4 fresh radishes, cut into thin rings

- 2 tablespoons toasted sunflower seeds

- 1 lemon, sliced

- 2 tablespoons finely chopped fresh parsley

- 2 tablespoons finely chopped fresh chives

- **Dressing:** 3 tablespoons of olive oil, juice of ½ lemon, 1 teaspoon Dijon mustard, 1 large clove garlic (minced), ground black pepper, and salt to taste, sea salt to taste.

Instructions:

Season the chicken breast with ground black pepper and salt to taste. Heat a non-stick pan to medium-high heat. Once it is hot, add olive oil. Put the chicken breast and cook for 4 - 5 minutes on each side. Set aside.

Meanwhile, make the dressing. Put olive oil, lemon juice, garlic, Dijon mustard, salt, and black pepper to taste in a small bowl. Whisk together until thoroughly mixed.

Put in a saucepan 2 cup of cold water, a pinch of salt, and the buckwheat and bring to the boil. Cover and simmer for 5 minutes on low heat. Then remove and rinse thoroughly with cold water and drained.

Mix the buckwheat, fresh mix salad, onion, radishes, and parsley in a deep glass bowl. Drizzle over the dressing and toss gently to mix. Cut the cooked chicken into thin strips and add them to the bowl. Sprinkle the salad with fresh chives and sunflower seeds. Serve salad immediately with slices of lemon.

30. Buckwheat with Broccoli and Grilled Chicken (gluten-free recipe)

Servings: 4

Ingredients:

- 2/3 cup raw buckwheat

- 5.5 oz (160 g) grilled chicken breast slices

- 1 cup fresh broccoli florets, chopped

- juice of ½ lemon

- 2 tablespoons olive oil

- 4 slices of lemon

- **Spices:** 2 tablespoons finely chopped fresh dill, ground black pepper to taste, salt to taste

Instructions:

Put in a saucepan 2 cups of cold water. Add salt and the buckwheat. Allow boiling for 5 minutes. Then remove and rinse thoroughly with cold water. Drain it into a colander. Set aside. Put in a saucepan 3 cups of hot water. Add salt, and broccoli florets boil for 2 - 3 minutes. Then drain, leave to cool.

Put the buckwheat, broccoli, lemon juice, olive oil, and all spices in a deep bowl and stir. At the top, arrange the chicken slices. Serve the salad immediately with slices of lemon.

31. Buckwheat with Smoked Ham

(gluten-free recipe)

Servings: 4

Ingredients:

- 2/3 cup raw buckwheat

- 1 fresh Iceberg lettuce

- 9 oz (255 g) thin-sliced smoked ham

- 8 cherry tomatoes, halved

- 1 English cucumber, cut into thin rings

- 1 small red onion, cut into thin rings

- **Dressing:** 2 finely chopped green onions, 2 tablespoons finely chopped parsley, 2 cloves crushed garlic, 4 tablespoons olive oil, juice of ½ lemon, ground black pepper to taste, sea salt to taste

Instructions:

Put in a saucepan 2 cups of cold water. Add salt and the buckwheat. Allow boiling for 5 minutes. Then remove and rinse thoroughly with cold water. Drain it into a colander. Set aside.

Meanwhile, make the dressing. Put olive oil, lemon juice, garlic, green onions, parsley, salt, and black pepper to taste in a small bowl. Whisk together until thoroughly mixed.

Tear the lettuce leaves. Add the onions, tomatoes, buckwheat, and cucumbers. Drizzle over the dressing and toss gently to mix.

Put the salad on a large serving plate. At the top, arrange the sliced smoked ham.

32. Buckwheat with Beetroot

(gluten-free recipe)

Servings: 4

Ingredients:

- ½ cup raw buckwheat

- 7 oz (200 g) fresh beetroot

- 1 fresh carrot, grated

- 1 small apple, grated

- **Spices:** juice of 1 lemon, 2 tablespoons olive oil, 1 tablespoon vinegar, 2 tablespoons finely chopped dill, 4 sprigs of dill for decoration, salt to taste, 4 lemon slices

Instructions:

Put buckwheat into a small saucepan and add 1.5 cups of water. Cover with a lid and bring to the boil. Once the water comes to the boil, turn the heat down to low and cook on a low heat until all the water has been absorbed. Once the water has been fully absorbed, rest the pot for another 10 minutes (with the lid firmly on) so that the buckwheat finishes cooking in its own steam. Once cooked, drain the buckwheat and set aside.

Place the beetroot in a pot with water and a pinch of salt, and 1 tablespoon of vinegar to boiling for 5 minutes. Drain it and let it cool. Grate the beetroot on a wholesale grater and mix with chopped dill. Put it in a deep bowl. Add the buckwheat, carrot, apple, and the spices, mix carefully.

Garnish each serving with a sprig of dill and lemon slice and serve the salad immediately.

Soups Recipes

R. Lazarova

This page intentionally left blank

33. Buckwheat and Red Lentils

(vegan, gluten-free recipe)

Servings: 4

Ingredients:

- 2/3 cup red lentils

- ½ cup raw buckwheat

- 2 cloves garlic, grated

- 1 red bell pepper, cut into cubes

- **Spices:** 2 teaspoon cumin powder, 1 teaspoon sweet paprika, sea salt to taste, 1 tablespoon olive oil

Instructions:

Rinse the lentils and buckwheat thoroughly with cold water.

Combine the red lentils, buckwheat, garlic, red bell pepper, cumin, and sweet paprika in a pot. Pour 4 cups hot water. Put the lid and cook over low - medium heat for 7 – 12 minutes. (Increase cooking time if necessary). Season the soup with salt to taste.

Serve it hot, drizzled with a little olive oil on top of each serving.

34. Mushrooms Soup with Buckwheat

(gluten-free recipe)

Servings: 4

Ingredients:

- 6 oz (170 g) fresh mushrooms, cut into small cubes

- 1/3 cup raw buckwheat

- 4 oz (115 g) fresh carrot, cut into small cubes

- 7 oz (200 g) russet potato, cut into small cubes

- 1 yellow onion, cut into small cubes

- 1 teaspoon butter + 1 tablespoon sunflower oil

- **Spices:** 1 bay leaf, a pinch ground black pepper, sea salt to taste, 1 tablespoon finely chopped parsley, 1 tablespoon chopped dill, 4 tablespoons lemon juice (at will)

Instructions:

Boil the buckwheat for 5 minutes in 1.5 cups of hot water. Drain the water and rinse thoroughly with cold water.

Heat the butter and sunflower oil in a pan. Put the carrot, potato, onion, and mushrooms in the hot butter. Sprinkle with black pepper and salt. Stir and continue to cook the ingredients together on low fire for 10 minutes. Then pour 4 cups hot water. Boil the soup for another 15 - 20 minutes. Add the buckwheat and bay leaf and cook soup on low fire for another 2 - 3 minutes. Remove the pot from the fire. Season with parsley and dill, mix. Serve the ready soup with lemon juice (at will).

35. Buckwheat Gazpacho

(gluten-free recipe)

Servings: 4

Ingredients:

- ½ cup raw buckwheat

- 1.5 lb (680 g) ripe Roma tomatoes, diced

- ½ handful of celery leaves

- 2 tablespoons shredded Cheddar cheese

- **Spices:** 1 tablespoon chopped walnuts, ½ teaspoon ground black pepper, salt to taste

Instructions:

Put in a saucepan 1.5 cups hot water. Add the buckwheat. Allow boiling for 5 minutes. Then remove and drain.

Put the tomatoes, celery, salt, and black pepper in a pot with a lid. Pour over 2 - 3 cups of cold water. Heat the mixture over medium-high heat. Once it is hot and cooks for 10 - 15 minutes.

Then remove the pan from the heat and put the soup in a food chopper. Chop soup in seconds.

Add the buckwheat and allow the soup to cool.

Sprinkle the soup with Cheddar cheese and walnuts.

36. *Pumpkin Cream Soup and Buckwheat*

(gluten-free recipe)

Servings: 4

Ingredients:

- 2 cup 100% Pumpkin Puree, canned – or one 15-oz can
- (or 14 oz - 400 g boiled pumpkin)
- 2/3 cup boiled buckwheat
- ½ tablespoon ginger root, cut into small pieces
- 2 fresh carrots, cut into small pieces
- 2 garlic cloves, cut into small pieces
- 3 tablespoons raw peeled pumpkin seeds
- 2 tablespoons sunflower oil
- ½ cup heavy cream
- **Spices:** a pinch clove - ground, a pinch nutmeg – ground, ground black pepper to taste, sea salt to taste

Instructions:

Bake the pumpkin seeds in a dry frying pan for 2 - 3 minutes over medium heat.

Heat the sunflower oil in a deep saucepan. Put the vegetables, mix them, and leave on low heat for 2 - 3 minutes. Pour 3 cups of hot water. When it boils, cook the vegetables for 20 minutes. Transfer the mixture into the container of a blender or processor. Process until desired consistency. Return mixture to saucepan. Add the pumpkin puree (or boiled pumpkin), the spices, and heavy cream, stir well. Bring to a boil, cover, reduce heat, and simmer 2 minutes more, stirring occasionally. Then add the buckwheat. Top each serving with pumpkin seeds.

37. Buckwheat Cream Soup with Carrots

(gluten-free recipe)

Servings: 4

Ingredients:

- ½ cup raw buckwheat

- 1 lb (450 g) fresh carrots, chopped

- 7 oz (200 g) russet potato, chopped

- 1 each fresh parsnip, chopped

- 3 sticks celery, chopped

- ½ tablespoon grated fresh ginger

- 2 tablespoons olive oil

- 1 teaspoon butter

- **Spices:** 2 tablespoons finely chopped parsley, ground black pepper to taste, salt to taste

Instructions:

Put in a saucepan 1.5 cups hot water. Add the

buckwheat. Allow boiling for 5 minutes. Then remove and drain.

Put the chopped carrots, potato, parsnip, celery, and ginger in a non-stick pot with preheated olive oil. Stir periodically and stew the vegetables on a low fire for 5 - 6 minutes. Add 4 cups hot water and salt, continue to cook the vegetables until soft. Add the buckwheat, cook soup on low fire for another 2 -3 minutes. Then by using a blender, blend the buckwheat soup into a homogeneous thick puree. Return the pot with soup on the cooking surface. Add ground black pepper and finely chopped parsley to the soup, mix.

Serve the ready soup puree in hot form; add 1/4 teaspoon butter to each serving.

38. Buckwheat Cream Soup with Spinach

(gluten-free recipe)

Servings: 4

Ingredients:

- ½ cup raw buckwheat

- 10.5 oz (310 g) fresh washed spinach leaves, chopped

- 1 sweet onion

- 2 garlic cloves

- 1 each russet potato

- 3 sticks celery

- 2 tablespoons sunflower oil

- 4 tablespoons Greek-style natural yogurt

- **Spices:** 2 tablespoons finely chopped parsley, 1 tablespoon finely chopped fresh dill, ground black pepper to taste, salt to taste

Instructions:

Peel the onions, garlic, potato, and celery, cut into cubes. Put in a non-stick pot with preheated olive oil. Stir periodically and stew on a low fire for a few minutes. Then add ground black pepper, salt, and 4 cups hot water. Bring to a boil. Let the vegetables cook over low heat for 20 minutes. Add the buckwheat and spinach, cook for another 5 minutes.

Then by using a blender, blend the buckwheat soup into a homogeneous thick puree. Return the pot with soup on the cooking surface. Add chopped parsley and chopped fresh dill to the soup, mix. Serve the ready soup puree in hot form, add 1-tablespoon Greek-style natural yogurt to each serving.

39. Buckwheat Broccoli Cream Soup

(gluten-free recipe)

Servings: 4

Ingredients:

- 2 cups fresh broccoli florets, chopped

- ½ cup buckwheat

- 7 oz (200 g) russet potato, cut into cubes

- 1 white onion, cut into cubes

- ½ cup heavy cream

- 2 tablespoons shredded Cheddar cheese

- **Spices:** 2 tablespoons finely chopped parsley, a pinch of grated nutmeg, ground black pepper to taste, salt to taste

Instructions:

In a saucepan, pour 1.5 cups hot water. Add salt and the buckwheat. Allow boiling for 5 minutes. Then remove and drain. Set aside.

In a stockpot, pour 3.5 cups of hot water and a pinch of salt. Add potatoes and onions. Bring to a boil. Let the vegetables cook over low heat for 20 minutes. Add the broccoli and grated nutmeg. Cook for another 5 minutes. Then by using a blender, blend the vegetables into a homogeneous thick puree. Return the pot with puree on the cooking surface. Add cream and buckwheat to the puree at this stage. Bring the soup to a boil, and then remove the stockpot from the fire. Add chopped parsley and mix.

Serve hot with ½ tablespoon shredded Cheddar cheese drizzled on top of each serving.

40. Buckwheat Beef Borscht

(gluten-free recipe)

Servings: 4

Ingredients:

- 11 oz (310 g) fresh beef stew meat

- ½ cup raw buckwheat

- 1 carrot, cut into small cubes

- 1 medium beet, cut into small cubes

- 2 garlic cloves, pressed

- 1 tablespoon tomato paste

- 1 cup fresh cabbage, cut into thin strips

- 2 ribs celery, cut into small cubes

- 2 tablespoons of sunflower oil

- 4 tablespoons sour cream, for garnish

- 1 teaspoon apple cider vinegar

- **Spices:** 1 - 2 bay leaves, a pinch ground black pepper, sea salt to taste, 1 tablespoon chopped dill

Instructions:

Boil the buckwheat for 5 minutes in 1.5 cups of hot. Set aside.

In a deep pot, add the meat and 4 - 5 cups of cold water. Bring it to a boil over low high heat, skimming off the scum. Then simmer it for about 1 hour.

Meanwhile, heat sunflower oil in a large skillet over medium-high heat. Add carrot, and cook 1 - 2 minutes. Then add the garlic and beets, cook for 1 - 2 minutes, stirring. Add apple cider vinegar, tomato paste, and 2 – 3 tablespoon of broth, cook for another 4 - 5 minutes, stirring frequently.

Add cabbage, celery, stewed vegetables, a pinch of ground black pepper, and 1-2 bay leaves in a pot. Stir occasionally, until meat is soft and beets are tender - about 30 minutes. Remove bay leaf and add the buckwheat. Continue to cook borscht on low fire for another 3 minutes. Remove the pot from the fire.

Serve with sour cream and dill.

41. Buckwheat Lamb Meatball Soup

(gluten-free recipe)

Servings: 4

Ingredients:

- **For meatball:**10.5 oz (300 g) fresh minced lamb, 1 egg white, a pinch of ground black pepper, a pinch of sea salt, ground coriander, ground cumin, dried oregano

- 2 tablespoons of sunflower oil

- 1 yellow onion, thinly sliced

- 2 garlic cloves, finely chopped

- 2 tablespoons tomato paste

- 4 – 5 cup vegetable or chicken broth

- 1/3 cup raw buckwheat

- **Spices:** 1 tablespoon finely chopped mint, 1 teaspoon sweet paprika, ground black pepper to taste

Instructions:

Boil the buckwheat for 3 minutes in 1.5 cups of hot

water. Then drain it and rinse it.

For the meatball: In a large plate, mix the minced lamb, 1 egg white, a pinch of ground black pepper, a pinch of sea salt, ¼ teaspoon ground coriander, ½ teaspoon ground cumin, ½ teaspoon dried oregano, 1 tablespoon finely chopped parsley. Form the mixture into small meatballs (the size of a hazelnut).

In a large pot, heat the sunflower oil over medium-high heat. Add the meatballs and cook, occasionally turning, until golden brown, 3 – 4 minutes. Transfer the meatballs to a plate.

Put to the same pot the onions, cooking and often stirring until it softened, 2 – 3 minutes. Add garlic, sweet paprika, ground black pepper to taste, tomato paste, and cook stirring continuously for about 1 minute. Add the broth and salt to taste and bring to a boil. Return the meatballs to the pot and return the soup to a simmer, 15 minutes. Then add the boiled buckwheat, bring it to a boil. Remove the pan after 2 minutes. Season the soup with finely chopped mint. Serve it warm.

42. Buckwheat Soup with Turkey Breast and Mushrooms

(gluten-free recipe)

Servings: 4

Ingredients:

- 4 tablespoons raw buckwheat

- 9 oz (250 g) fresh boneless, skinless turkey breast fillet, cut into small cubes

- 3.5 oz (100 g) fresh mushrooms, sliced

- 1 yellow onion, cut into small cubes

- 1 large carrot, cut into small cubes

- 2 garlic cloves, cut into small cubes

- 1 tablespoon sunflower oil + 2 teaspoons butter

- 1 cup of coconut milk

- 4 cup chicken broth (or hot water)

- **Spices:** 6 - 7 peppercorns, 1 bay leaf, 2 tablespoons finely chopped parsley, ground black pepper to taste, and salt to taste

Instructions:

In a large pot, heat the sunflower oil + butter over medium-high heat. Add the onion, carrot, turkey breast, mushrooms, and cook for 3 - 4 minutes, turning occasionally. Add the broth, salt, 6 - 7 peppercorns, and bring to a boil. Cook the soup until meat is soft, about 30 minutes.

Then pour coconut milk, add bay leaf and the buckwheat. Continue to cook soup on low fire for another 5 – 6 minutes. Remove the pot from the fire.

Serve the soup warm, sprinkled with ground black pepper and parsley.

43. Chicken Soup with Buckwheat Pasta

(gluten-free recipe)

Servings: 4

Ingredients:

- 9 oz (255 g) boneless, skinless chicken breasts, cut into small cubes

- 3 oz (85 g) Buckwheat pasta

- 1 tablespoon wholemeal Buckwheat flour

- 1 yellow onion, chopped

- 2 celery ribs, chopped

- 1 large fresh carrot, chopped

- ½ cup cream

- 2 tablespoons sunflower oil or 1 teaspoon of butter

- **Spices:** juice of ½ lemon, a pinch of dried thyme, 1 tablespoon finely chopped parsley, ground black pepper to taste, salt to taste

Instructions:

In a large pot, heat the sunflower oil + butter over medium-high heat. Add the onion, celery, carrot, chicken, and cook for 3 - 4 minutes, turning occasionally. Add the 4 – 5 cup hot water, salt, and bring to a boil. Cook the soup until meat is soft, about 30 minutes. In a small bowl, put the flour; add a few tablespoons of cold water under constant stirring until a homogeneous mixture. Add it in the pot stirring continuously. Bring to a boil. Add the Buckwheat pasta, stir and reduce heat, simmer uncovered 6 -7 minutes. Then add cream, thyme, and parsley, mix and remove the pot from the heat. Season the soup with ground black pepper. Serve it warm. Add lemon juice to taste.

44. Buckwheat Soup with Chicken Breast

(gluten-free recipe)

Servings: 4

Ingredients:

- 11 oz (310 g) Boneless Skinless Chicken Breast

- 2 oz (56 g) buckwheat groats

- 7 oz (200 g) russet potato, diced

- 1 medium carrot, diced

- 1 small onion, diced

- 1 tablespoon olive oil

- **Spices***:* salt to taste, ground white pepper to taste, 2 tablespoons finely chopped parsley, 1 tablespoon finely chopped dill, 1 bay leaf

Instructions:

Wash the chicken breast thoroughly with cold water. Then put them in a pot with the cold water and bring to a boil. Reduce the heat and simmer for 25 – 30 minutes. Then transfer the chicken breast to a plate. When cool, cut into small cubes, set aside.

Add the potato, carrot, onion, bay leaf, and buckwheat groats into the chicken broth. Cook over low heat for 25 minutes. Return the chicken breast to the broth, bring to a boil. Remove the pot from the fire after 1 minute. Add ground white pepper, salt, finely chopped parsley, and dill, mix.

Serve the soup warm into a deep bowl, add a few drops of olive oil.

45. Buckwheat Noodles and Fish Soup

(gluten-free recipe)

Servings: 4

Ingredients:

- 11 oz (310 g) fresh skinless fish fillet (cod)

- 3 oz (85 g) buckwheat noodles

- 1 sweet onion, finely chopped

- 1 tablespoon grated ginger root

- 2 cloves crushed garlic, finely chopped

- 2 - 3 sweet mini red peppers, finely chopped

- 1 jalapeno pepper, finely chopped

- 2 tablespoons vegetable oil

- **Spices:** salt to taste, ground white pepper to taste, 2 tablespoons finely chopped parsley, juice of 1 lime

Instructions:

Wash the fish with cold water, cut it into small pieces.

In a large pot, heat the vegetable oil over medium-high heat. Add the onion, ginger, garlic, mini red peppers, jalapeno pepper, and cook, turning occasionally, 3 - 4 minutes. Add 4 cups hot water, salt and cook about 15 minutes. Then add fish and buckwheat noodles. Continue to cook soup on low fire, occasionally stirring, for another 5 – 6 minutes. Remove the pot from the fire.

Serve the soup with finely chopped parsley and sprinkled with white pepper. Season with lime juice to taste.

Main Dishes Recipes

This page intentionally left blank

46. Buckwheat and Portabella Mushrooms Casserole (gluten-free recipe)

Servings: 4

Ingredients:

- 1 cup uncooked buckwheat groats

- 6 oz (170 g) fresh portabella mushrooms, sliced

- 1 yellow onion, chopped

- 1 carrot, finely chopped

- 3 eggs

- 3.5oz (100 g) cream for cooking

- 5oz (140 g) Cheddar cheese, grated

- 3 - 4 tablespoons vegetable oil

- **Spices:** 3 tablespoons finely chopped fresh dill, sea salt to taste, ground black pepper to taste

Instructions:

Rinse the buckwheat and put it in a pot with 2.5 cups of cold water. Bring to a boil. Cover the pot and simmer for 3 minutes after boiling point. Turn off the heat, add a pinch of salt and let it sit for 10 more minutes. Then stir vigorously, set aside.

In a frying pan, heat the oil over low heat. Add the onion, carrot, and mushrooms, season with ground black pepper, and salt. Cook mixture, occasionally turning, 3 - 4 minutes. Add fresh dill and stir.

In a deep bowl, beat the eggs with a pinch of salt and add the cream.

Preheat the oven to 390 F / 200 C.

In glass casserole, baking dish, pour half the porridge, then add the mixture with the onion, carrot, dill, and mushrooms. Then pour the remaining porridge. Top pour the egg mixture; sprinkle the cheese. Bake the dish for 25 minutes; turn off the oven; let it inside until the cheese is golden brown.

Serve the dish warm.

47. Vegan Buckwheat Patties

(vegan, gluten-free recipe)

Servings: 4

Ingredients:

- 1 ½ cups uncooked buckwheat groats

- 2 fresh medium carrots, grated

- 1 small sweet onion, grated

- 2 red sweet mini peppers, finely chopped

- 1 - 2 tablespoons olive oil

- **Spices:** thyme to taste, 1 teaspoon dried oregano, 2 tablespoons finely chopped parsley, sea salt to taste, ground black pepper to taste

Instructions:

Rinse the buckwheat groats. In a saucepan, combine the buckwheat groats with 3 cups of water. Bring to a boil, reduce the heat, and let simmer until all the water is absorbed. This should take less than 3 - 4 minutes. Set aside in a large bowl until cool.

Add carrots, onion, peppers, olive oil, and all spices into the buckwheat, mix gently. Take some of the mixture and roll it into a ball. Transfer it onto a baking tray lined with parchment paper. Press down until you get the desired thickness. Repeat with the rest of the mixture.

Preheat the oven to 355 F / 180 C.

Bake in the oven for 20 – 30 minutes until patties are brown.

Serve with fresh salad or guacamole.

48. Buckwheat Potato Burger with Cheddar Cheese

Servings: 4 - 6

Ingredients:

- 1 lb (450 g) russet baking potatoes

- 1 ½ cups uncooked buckwheat groats

- 2 fresh medium carrots, grated

- 1 - 2 tablespoons oatmeal

- 1 tablespoon breadcrumbs

- 1 - 2 tablespoons olive oil

- 8 oz (225 g) sliced Cheddar cheese

- **Spices:** 1 teaspoon dried oregano, 2 tablespoons finely chopped parsley, sea salt to taste, ground black pepper to taste

- **For garnish:** avocado, lettuce leaves, tomato, and parsley

- **4 – 6 buns**

Instructions:

Pour oatmeal with hot water, set aside until cool.

In a saucepan, combine the buckwheat groats with 3 cups of water. Bring to a boil, reduce the heat, and let simmer until all the water is absorbed. This should take less than 3 - 4 minutes. Set aside in a large bowl until cool.

Heat olive oil in a pot over medium-high heat. Add the carrot, saute it for 1 – 2 minutes, set aside until cool.

Peel the potatoes and cut them into small pieces. Place them in a pot and pour in 3 – 4 cups water. Cover with lid and bring to a boil. Cook about 10 – 15 minutes until soft. Then drain them, set aside until cool.

Transfer the potatoes into a mixing bowl. Mash them with a potato masher or fork. Add carrot, buckwheat, oatmeal, breadcrumbs, and all spices; mix gently. Form mixture into patties.

Preheat grill to medium heat. Use Non- flammable cooking spray to grease the grill.

Place the patties on the grill for 5 - 6 minutes per side until a crust on both sides. Turn with appropriate tongs (in no case, do not use a fork). In the last minute of grilling, add a slice of Cheddar cheese to each patty and let the cheese melt.

Split each bun and place a patty in the middle. Garnish with avocado, lettuce leaves, tomato, and parsley.

Place the burgers on a platter and serve with your favorite sauce.

49. Spicy Buckwheat Croquettes with Mushrooms

Servings: 4

Ingredients:

- 1 cup uncooked buckwheat groats

- 5 oz (150 g) mushrooms, finely chopped

- 9 oz (255 g) boiled russet potato, grated

- 1 egg

- 2 fresh medium carrots, grated

- 1 small sweet onion, finely chopped

- 1 – 2 cloves garlic, grated

- 1 jalapeno pepper (optional), finely chopped

- 1 - 2 tablespoons sunflower oil + 1 teaspoon butter

- **Spices:** ½ teaspoon cumin, a pinch of nutmeg, 1 tablespoon finely chopped fresh dill, 2 tablespoons finely chopped parsley, sea salt to taste, ground black pepper to taste

- **Coating:** 2 eggs – slightly beaten, ½ cup cornflour, 4 -

5 tablespoons plain dry breadcrumbs, a pinch of salt, a pinch of ground black pepper, 4 - 5 tablespoons sunflower oil for frying

Instructions:

Rinse the buckwheat groats. In a saucepan, combine the buckwheat groats with 3 cups of water. Bring to a boil, reduce the heat, and let simmer until all the water is absorbed. This should take less than 4 minutes. Set aside in a large bowl until cool.

Heat sunflower oil or 1 teaspoon of butter in a non-stick pan over medium-high heat. Saute carrots, onion, a jalapeno pepper (optional), mushrooms, all spices, and garlic for 3 – 4 minutes. Let them cool. Then add the potato and the buckwheat. Stir the whole mixture together with the egg. With greased hands, shape the croquettes.

Whisk together two eggs. Season the cornflour with salt and pepper in a flat dish. Place the breadcrumbs in a wide, shallow bowl.

Heat 4 - 5 tablespoons sunflower oil in a wide pot or skillet over medium-high heat. Roll the croquettes in cornflour first, then in the egg, then in the breadcrumbs. Fry about 6 -7 minutes per side until golden and crisp.

R. Lazarova

Serve hot with fresh vegetable salad.

50. Vegetable Buckwheat Stew

(vegan, gluten-free recipe)

Servings: 4

Ingredients:

- 1 cup uncooked buckwheat groats

- 1 yellow onion

- 1 fresh carrot

- ½ green bell pepper

- 2 ribs fresh celery

- 4 Roma tomatoes

- ½ cup peas, canned

- 3 tablespoons of sunflower oil

- **Spices:** 2 teaspoons sweet paprika, 1 tablespoon tomato paste, 2 tablespoons finely chopped parsley, salt to taste

Instructions:

Clean, wash and chop all the vegetables into small pieces.

In a deep pan, heat the sunflower oil over low heat. Add the chopped vegetables. Saute 4 - 5 minutes, turning occasionally. Season with sweet paprika and a pinch of salt. Stir, add tomato paste, tomatoes, peas, buckwheat, and 2.5 - 3 cups hot water. Allow the dish to simmer for 4 – 5 minutes on low heat until the mixture thickens. Remove the pan from the heat; add the parsley and salt.

The dish can be served both - hot and cold.

51. Buckwheat with Tomato Sauce and Basil

(gluten-free recipe)

Servings: 4

Ingredients:

- 1 cup uncooked buckwheat groats

- 1.5 lb (680 g) ripe Roma tomatoes, or 1 can – 14.5 oz (410 g) diced tomatoes

- 2 - 3 cloves garlic, grated

- 2 - 3 tablespoons olive oil

- 1 teaspoon brown sugar

- 4 tablespoons Mozzarella cheese, shredded

- **Spices:** 10 fresh basil leaves, ground black pepper to taste, sea salt to taste

Instructions:

Rinse the buckwheat and put it in a pot with 2.5 cups of cold water. Bring to a boil. Cover the pot and simmer for 3 minutes, after boiling point (or until water is absorbed). Turn off the heat, add a pinch of salt and let it sit for 10 more minutes.

Meanwhile, in a deep saucepan, heat the olive oil over low heat. Put the finely chopped garlic, tomatoes, pinch of salt, black pepper, and sugar. Simmer the sauce until thickened, add the buckwheat, basil leaves, and mix well. Remove the pan from the heat. Sprinkle each serving with 1-tablespoon Mozzarella cheese.

52. Buckwheat with Broccoli and Cream

(gluten-free recipe)

Servings: 4

Ingredients:

- 12 oz (340 g) fresh broccoli florets

- 1 cup uncooked buckwheat groats

- 3.5 oz (100 g) cottage cheese

- ½ cup sour cream

- 2 tablespoons sliced green olives

- *Spices:* 1 teaspoon curry powder, 2 tablespoons chopped dill, ground black pepper to taste, salt to taste, 1 teaspoon sweet paprika

Instructions:

Rinse the buckwheat and put it in a pot with 2.5 cups of cold water. Bring to a boil. Cover the pot and simmer for 3 - 4 minutes after boiling point (or until water is absorbed). Turn off the heat, and let it sit for 4 - 5 more minutes.

Rinse the broccoli florets. Put in a deep saucepan with 3

cups of hot water, add broccoli. Put the lid on the pan so that the broccoli will keep its fresh green colour. After 5 minutes, remove the pan off the heat, drain.

In a deep bowl, crush the broccoli, add cream, cottage cheese, curry powder, black pepper, dill, olives, and the buckwheat. Mix well.

Serve the dish, sprinkle with sweet paprika.

53. Buckwheat with Sweet Peas

(vegan, gluten-free recipe)

Servings: 4

Ingredients:

- 1 cup uncooked buckwheat groats

- 1 can 15 oz (425 g) sweet peas

- 1 carrot, finely chopped

- 1 sweet onion, finely chopped

- 2 tablespoons olive oil

- 3 cup hot chicken broth

- **Spices**: 1 tablespoon finely chopped fresh dill, 1 tablespoon finely chopped fresh mint leaves, sea salt to taste

Instructions:

Rinse the buckwheat groats, set aside.

Rinse the peas thoroughly with cold water. Drain it well, set aside.

In a deep pan, heat the olive oil over medium heat. Add the onion and carrot, cook for 2 minutes. Add hot chicken stock and buckwheat groats. Let simmer for about 7 minutes, or the buckwheat is al dente, and most of the broth has absorbed. Then add sweet peas, salt, and dill. Mix well and remove the pan when the dish is still loose, and there is a little liquid remaining. The buckwheat will continue to absorb, so this just prevents the dish from getting gluggy.

Serve the dish after 10 – 15 minutes. Add mint leaves to each serving.

54. Stuffed Buckwheat Peppers

(gluten-free recipe)

Servings: 4

Ingredients:

- 1 cup uncooked buckwheat groats

- 4 red bell peppers or mixed bell peppers

- 1 fresh carrot, finely chopped

- 1 yellow onion, finely chopped

- 2 - 3 ripe Roma tomatoes, cut into rings

- 3 tablespoons sunflower oil

- 3 ½ cups hot chicken broth (or vegetable broth)

- 8 tablespoons natural Greek yogurt

- **Spices:** 2 tablespoons finely chopped parsley, ground black pepper to taste, salt to taste

Instructions:

Rinse the buckwheat groats, set aside.

Cut the peppers in half lengthwise and remove all seeds. Rinse them thoroughly with cold water. Drain it well, set aside.

In a deep pan, heat the sunflower oil over medium heat. Add the onion and carrot, cook, until softened for about 2 – 3 minutes. Add buckwheat and 3 cups chicken broth and bring to a boil, then turn the heat down and simmer for 4 minutes or until buckwheat absorbs the liquid. Cover the pot and turn off the heat. After 10 minutes, add parsley, ground black pepper, salt, and mix thoroughly.

Preheat the oven to 390 F / 200 C.

Place all pepper halves in a baking dish. Spoon the buckwheat mixture into each pepper half and stuff it. Top with 2 – 3 rings tomato. Pour ½-cup chicken broth and bake the dish for about 20 – 30 minutes.

Serve each serving of stuffed peppers with 2 tablespoons yogurt.

55. *Vegan Stuffed Zucchini with Buckwheat*

(vegan, gluten-free recipe)

Servings: 4

Ingredients:

- 2.5 lb (1 kg 150 g) fresh zucchini

- 1 cup uncooked buckwheat groats

- 1 yellow onion, finely chopped

- 1 clove of garlic, grated

- 2 - 3 tablespoons sunflower oil

- **Spices:** 2 tablespoons finely chopped parsley, 2 tablespoons finely chopped fresh dill,

  ¼ teaspoon ground black pepper, sea salt to taste

Instructions:

Rinse the buckwheat groats, set aside.

Cut the caps off your zucchinis and hollow them out using a spoon (about 5 mm thick all around). Rinse and dry them, season with salt, set aside.

In a saucepan, heat the sunflower oil over medium heat. Saute the onion until softened for about 1 – 2 minutes. Add buckwheat and 2 cups of hot water. Bring to a boil. Reduce the heat and let simmer until the water is absorbed. This should take less than 3 minutes. Add parsley, 1-tablespoon fresh dill, salt, black pepper, and garlic, stir. Remove from heat.

Stuff the zucchini with buckwheat stuffing and close with their caps. Place them in a pot (Spread any left-over stuffing in the middle of the pot, between the zucchini). Add a cup of water and bring to a boil. Reduce the heat, put the lid, and let the dish simmer for about 15 minutes. Remove the pot from the heat.

After 10 – 15 minutes, serve the zucchinis with sauce obtained during the cooking. Sprinkle with 1-tablespoon fresh dill.

56. Stuffed Eggplant with Buckwheat and Chickpeas (gluten-free recipe)

Servings: 4

Ingredients:

- 2 large eggplant

- 2/3 cup uncooked buckwheat groats

- ½ can 8 oz (225 g) chickpeas

- 4.5 oz (125 g) sliced fresh mushrooms

- 1 yellow onion, finely chopped

- 2 cloves of garlic, grated

- 2 - 3 tablespoons sunflower oil

- 4 oz (115 g) shredded Mozzarella cheese

- 1 can - 14 oz (450 g) pettite diced tomatoes in tomato juice

- 2 tablespoons finely chopped parsley

- **Spices**: 2 tablespoons finely chopped parsley, ½ handful fresh basil leaves, ¼ teaspoon ground black pepper, sea salt to taste

Instructions:

Rinse and drain chickpeas. Set aside.

In a bowl, combine tomatoes, 2 tablespoons parsley, and a pinch of salt. Set aside.

Cut into two halves length the eggplant. Scoop out the flesh of it. Season shells with salt and set aside.

Rinse the buckwheat groats. In a saucepan, combine the buckwheat groats with 2 cups of water. Bring to a boil, reduce the heat, and let simmer until all the water is absorbed. This should take less than 3 minutes. Set aside in a large bowl.

Heat sunflower oil in a deep pan over medium-high heat. Saute onion, mushrooms, and garlic for about 5 – 6 minutes. Stir and season with salt and pepper. Add the mixture, chickpeas, and all spices to the buckwheat, mix until everything is well combined.

Preheat the oven to 390 F / 200 C.

Place all eggplant halves in a casserole-baking dish. Spoon the buckwheat mixture into each eggplant half and stuff it. Pour with tomato mixture and bake about 30 - 40 minutes. Then sprinkle top with Mozzarella cheese. Bake the dish until it is evenly brown.

Serve each stuffed eggplant with 2 - 3 tablespoons tomato sauce.

57. Buckwheat with Leeks

(vegan, gluten-free recipe)

Servings: 4

Ingredients:

- 1 cup uncooked buckwheat groats

- 2 – 3 fresh leeks (white part only), halved lengthwise and sliced into half rings

- 2 small fresh carrots, cut into thin rings

- 3 cups hot chicken broth

- 3 tablespoons sunflower oil

- ½ cup white wine

- **Spices:** 1 teaspoon sweet paprika, 1 teaspoon dried savory, 2 tablespoons finely chopped parsley, sea salt to taste, ground black pepper to taste

Instructions:

Rinse the buckwheat groats, set aside.

Heat sunflower oil in a deep pot over medium-high

heat. Add the carrots and leeks. Cook, occasionally stirring for 7 – 8 minutes until softened. Then add sweet paprika and buckwheat to the pot. Stir about ½ minute. Add the wine, stir and let simmer until it is completely absorbed. At this point, ladle in the chicken broth about ½ cup at a time, keeping the mixture at a low simmer. At the liquid starts to get absorbed by the buckwheat, add a bit more to the pot until used all 3 cups, and it is being absorbed entirely by the buckwheat. Add salt, black pepper, savory, and parsley; stir to combine.

58. Buckwheat with Mushrooms

(gluten-free recipe)

Servings: 4

Ingredients:

- 1 cup uncooked buckwheat groats

- 7 oz (200 g) fresh mushrooms

- 1 white onion, finely chopped

- 2 small fresh carrots, finely chopped

- 3 cups vegetable broth or water

- 2 tablespoons sunflower oil

- ½ tablespoon butter

- **Spices:** 1 tablespoon finely chopped fresh dill, 2 tablespoons finely chopped parsley, sea salt to taste, ground black pepper to taste

Instructions:

Rinse the buckwheat groats with cold water in a colander, drain. In a saucepan, combine the buckwheat groats with 3 cups of vegetable broth or water. Bring to a boil, reduce the heat, and let simmer until all the water is absorbed. This should take less than 3 - 4 minutes. Set aside.

Clean the mushrooms with kitchen paper and cut them into small pieces.

Heat sunflower oil and butter in the frying pan or wok. Add onion and carrots, cook on low heat for 4 - 5 minutes. Stir often. Add the mushrooms and continue cooking for about 6 – 7 minutes. Then season with salt and ground black pepper to taste.

Add the buckwheat, dill, and parsley to the pan and mix well. Serve immediately.

59. Buckwheat and Brown Rice Patties

(vegan, gluten-free recipe)

Servings: 4

Ingredients:

- 1 cup uncooked buckwheat groats

- 1 cup of brown rice

- 7 oz (200 g) fresh washed spinach leaves

- 1 yellow onion, finely chopped

- 2 cloves of garlic, grated

- 3 - 4 tablespoons sunflower oil

- 3 - 4 tablespoons breadcrumbs, gluten-free

- **Spices:** 1 teaspoon cumin powder, 1 tablespoon finely chopped dill, 2 tablespoons finely chopped parsley, sea salt to taste, ground black pepper to taste

Instructions:

Heat 1-tablespoon sunflower oil in a saucepan over medium-high heat. Saute the spinach with a pinch of salt for 1

- 2 minutes. Set aside.

Rinse the buckwheat groats. In a saucepan, combine the buckwheat groats with 2.5 cups of water. Bring to a boil, reduce the heat, and let simmer until all the water is absorbed. This should take less than 5 minutes. Set aside in a large bowl until cool.

Heat 2 tablespoons sunflower oil in a non – stick pot over medium-high heat. Saute onion, garlic, and rice for 2 – 3 minutes. Add 2.5 cups of hot water and salt. Bring to a boil, reduce the heat, and let simmer until all the water is absorbed. Let him soak up the water thoroughly. Set aside in a large bowl until cool.

Combine in a deep bowl, the buckwheat, rice, spinach, and all spices. Cover the bowl with plastic food wrap and refrigerate for 1 hour. Then grease your hands with oil, take some of the mixture and roll it into a ball. Roll the ball in breadcrumbs. Then transfer it on to a baking tray lined with parchment paper. Press down until you get the desired thickness. Repeat with the rest of the mixture.

Preheat the oven to 355 F / 180 C. Bake the patties in the oven for 20 minutes. Serve them hot. Garnish the patties with natural yogurt.

60. Stewed Beef with Buckwheat

(gluten-free recipe)

Servings: 4

Ingredients:

- 21 oz (600 g) boneless fresh diced beef

- ½ cup uncooked buckwheat groats

- 1 medium carrot, chopped

- 1 red bell pepper, chopped

- 2 cloves of garlic, chopped

- 3 tablespoons sunflower oil

- **Spices:** 2 teaspoons ground cumin, 1 tablespoon sweet paprika, 2 tablespoons chopped parsley, ground black pepper to taste, 1 teaspoon crushed red pepper (at will), salt to taste

Instructions:

Rinse buckwheat under cold water. Set aside.

By using a blender, blend the carrots, peppers, and

garlic into a homogeneous mixture.

In a deep pan, heat the sunflower oil over medium heat. Add the diced beef, and stew for 4 - 5 minutes, turning it occasionally. Add vegetable mixture to the beef. Stir well, add the sweet paprika, cumin, black pepper, and crushed red pepper (at will). Pour the mixture with 2 - 2.5 cups of hot water. Reduce the heat and let the dish simmer over low heat. After 1 hour, add the buckwheat and continue cooking until the meat softens (5 - 8 minutes). Add chopped parsley and salt to taste, mix. Serve the dish warm.

61. Buckwheat Meatballs with Beef and Sauce (gluten-free recipe)

Servings: 4

Ingredients:

- ½ cup uncooked buckwheat groats

- 14 oz (400 g) beef mince, 12 % fat

- 1 egg

- **Spices:** 1 tablespoon green onion, finely chopped, 2 teaspoon ground cumin, 1 teaspoon sweet paprika, 1 teaspoon dried thyme, 2 tablespoons finely chopped parsley, 1.5 teaspoon Worcester sauce, ground black pepper to taste, 1 teaspoon crushed red pepper (at will), salt to taste

Instructions:

Rinse buckwheat under cold water. In a saucepan, combine the buckwheat with 1 ½ cups of water. Bring to a boil. Reduce the heat to low and simmer 10 minutes. Put the lid and set aside. After 15 minutes, fluff cooked buckwheat with a fork; add to the beef mince, egg, and all spices. Mix until everything is well combined.

Shape meatballs from the mixture with your hands and flatten them carefully. The number of meatballs depends on their size. Place the meatballs on a plate. Refrigerate for 10 - 15 minutes. Meanwhile, **prepare the sauce:** 2 tablespoons sunflower oil, 1 yellow onion, 1 small fresh carrot, 1 - 2 garlic cloves, 1.5 cups tomatoes finely chopped, 2 tablespoons finely chopped parsley, 1.5 cups warm beef broth (or water).

Heat sunflower oil over medium heat in a non-stick pan. Finely chop the onion, carrot, and garlic. Add in the pan; stir well. After 2 minutes, add the tomatoes, cook 4 -5 minutes. Then add hot beef broth and the meatballs. Put the lid and simmer 20 minutes. Then turn over the meatballs and cook for another 20 minutes. Remove the pan from the heat.

Serve meatballs with sauce warm, sprinkle with finely chopped parsley.

62. Oven Baked Beef Stew with Buckwheat

(gluten-free recipe)

Servings: 4

Ingredients:

- 21 oz (600 g) boneless fresh diced beef

- 1 cup uncooked buckwheat groats

- 1 yellow onion, chopped

- 1 can – 14.5 oz (410 g) diced tomatoes in tomato juice

- 3 tablespoons sunflower oil

- **Spices:** a pinch of dried tarragon, fresh thyme to taste, ground black pepper to taste, salt to taste

Instructions:

Rinse buckwheat under cold water. In a saucepan, combine the buckwheat with 2 ½ cups of water. Bring to a boil. Reduce the heat to low and simmer 10 minutes. Put it in the baking tray in which it will be baked, and set aside.

In a deep saucepan, heat the oil over medium heat. Add the onions to caramelize for 2 - 3 minutes. Then add the meat, stir and, cook for a few minutes. Pour with 2 - 3 cups of hot water. Bring to low heat until the meat softens. Transfer it to the tray with buckwheat; add the tomatoes and all spices. Mix.

Preheat the oven to 390 F / 200 C.

Put the baking tray in the oven. The dish should be baked for 5 - 10 minutes. Turn off the oven and leave the baking tray for 10 minutes. Serve the dish warm with a beetroot salad.

For the salad: 13 oz (350 g) beetroot, 1 large carrot, 1 tablespoon finely chopped parsley, juice of ½ lemon, 2 tablespoons olive oil, salt to taste.

Peel the beetroot and carrot, wash them and grate them on a grater. Add the spices and stir.

63. Buckwheat Casserole with Pork

(gluten-free recipe)

Servings: 4

Ingredients:

- 18 oz (500 g) minced pork, 10% fat

- 1 cup uncooked buckwheat groats

- 1 yellow onion, chopped

- 1 fresh medium carrot

- 1 cup whole milk

- 2 eggs

- 3 tablespoons grated Cheddar cheese

- 3 tablespoons sunflower oil

- **Spices:** a pinch of dried oregano, 2 tablespoons finely chopped parsley, ground black pepper to taste, salt to taste

Instructions:

Rinse buckwheat under cold water. In a saucepan, combine the buckwheat with 2 ½ cups of water. Bring to a boil. Reduce the heat to low and simmer 3 - 4 minutes. Put it in the casserole-baking dish in which it will be baked, and set aside.

In a deep saucepan, heat the oil over medium heat. Add the onions to caramelize for 2 - 3 minutes. Then add the minced pork and all spices; stir and put it on top of buckwheat.

In a deep bowl, mix eggs, milk, and salt. Beat the resulting mass. Then pour the buckwheat with minced pork. Leave to brew for 5 - 6 minutes. Pour the mixture into a casserole baking dish, sprinkle with cheese.

Preheat the oven to 390 F / 200 C.

Put the dish in the oven for 15 – 20 minutes.

Serve the ready dish warm with fresh salad.

64. Pork Roll and Buckwheat Sauce

Servings: 4

Ingredients:

- 1.8 lb (815 g) minced pork, 10% fat

- 1 egg

- 1 slice bread (cut into cubes)

- 1 onion, finely chopped

- ½ cup celery, finely chopped

- 1 carrot, finely grated

- 2 garlic cloves, finely grated

- 4 - 5 tablespoons cheddar cheese, grated

- 1 tablespoon butter

- **Spices:** 2 tablespoons finely chopped parsley, 1 teaspoon Dijon mustard, ground black pepper to taste, a pinch of grated nutmeg, salt to taste

    For the sauce: ½ cup uncooked buckwheat groats, 1 can – 14.5 oz (410 g) diced tomatoes in tomato juice, 2 tablespoons vegetable oil, 1 teaspoon oregano, 2 cloves garlic - crushed, ground black pepper to taste, salt to taste

Instructions:

Process bread in a blender or food processor until fine crumbs form. Transfer to a deep bowl. Add minced pork, egg, onion, celery, carrot, garlic, and all spices. Mix well and process until smooth.

Spread the mixture on the baking paper. Shape the meat mixture into a rectangle. Top with the butter and cheese to within 0.5 inches (1.5 cm) of the edge. Roll up jelly-roll style, starting with a short side, pinch to seal edges. Place seam side down in a greased baking tray.

Preheat the oven to 350 F / 180 C.

Bake the meat roll for 80 – 90 minutes. Let stand for 10 minutes before serving. Then cut it into thick slices about 1inch (2.5 cm).

For the sauce: Rinse buckwheat under cold water. In a saucepan, combine the buckwheat with 1.5 cups of water. Bring to a boil. Reduce the heat to low and simmer 10 minutes. Set aside.

In a frying pan, heat the vegetable oil, add the tomatoes, garlic, pepper, and salt to taste. Let the sauce simmer for about 10 minutes. Then add buckwheat and oregano, stir. Pour each portion of meat with the sauce.

65. Stew Pork, Leeks, and Buckwheat

(gluten-free recipe)

Servings: 4

Ingredients:

- 1.5 lb (680 g) pork stew meat boneless

- 1 cup uncooked buckwheat groats

- 14 oz (400 g) fresh leeks, finely chopped

- 1 tablespoon tomato paste

- 3 - 3.5 cups chicken or vegetable broth (or hot water)

- 3 tablespoons sunflower oil

- ½ cup white wine

- **Spices:** 2 teaspoons sweet paprika, 2 tablespoons finely chopped parsley, ground black pepper to taste, salt to taste

Instructions:

Rinse buckwheat under cold water. Set aside. In a deep pan, heat the sunflower oil over medium heat. Add the meat and stew for 4 - 5 minutes, turning it occasionally. Add chopped leeks and saute 3 - 4 minutes. Then add the sweet paprika, black pepper, tomato paste, and white wine. Cook 3 – 4 minutes and pour broth (or hot water). Reduce the heat and let the dish simmer over low heat. After 1 – 1.5 hours, add the buckwheat and continue cooking until the meat softens. Add chopped parsley and salt to taste, mix.

66. *Chicken with White Pearl Onions and Buckwheat (gluten-free recipe)*

Servings: 4

Ingredients:

- ½ cup uncooked buckwheat groats

- 1.6 lb (725 g) boneless, skinless chicken breasts

- 5 oz (145 g) white pearl onions

- 2 cloves of garlic, finely chopped

- 1 tablespoon grated fresh ginger

- 3 fresh Roma tomatoes, cut into small cubes

- 3 tablespoons sunflower oil

- 2 cups chicken broth (or hot water)

- **Spices:** 1 - 2 bay leaf, ground black pepper, and salt to taste, 2 tablespoons finely chopped parsley, 2 tablespoons finely chopped fresh chives

Instructions:

Rinse buckwheat under cold water. Set aside.

Chop the chicken breasts into pieces about 1 inch (2 cm). In a deep pan, heat the sunflower oil over medium heat. Add the chicken, and stew for 4 - 5 minutes, turning it occasionally. Then add the white pearl onions, the garlic, and the ginger. Allow the mixture to stew 3 - 4 minutes and add the tomatoes. Stir and pour over the mixture with chicken broth (or hot water). Cook the dish over low heat for 40 minutes or until the meat softens. Add the buckwheat groats; continue cooking for another 7 - 8 minutes. Season it with salt, pepper to taste, and parsley. Mix and serve each portion sprinkled with finely chopped chives.

67. Buckwheat with Chicken and Soy Sauce

Servings: 4

Ingredients:

- 2/3 cup uncooked buckwheat groats

- 1.4 lb (640 g) mini chicken breast fillets

- 1 white onion, chopped

- 1 fresh carrot, cut into long thin strips

- ½ green bell pepper, cut into long thin strips

- 1 jalapeno or serrano pepper, finely chopped (at will)

- 2 tablespoons sunflower oil

- 1 - 2 tablespoons soy sauce

- 2.5 - 3 cups hot chicken broth (or hot water)

- **Spices:** ground black pepper to taste, salt to taste, 2 tablespoons finely chopped parsley

Instructions:

Rinse buckwheat under cold water. Set aside.

In a deep pan, heat the sunflower oil over medium heat. Add the chicken, and stew for 3 minutes, turning it occasionally. Then add the carrot, onion, green bell pepper, jalapeno, or serrano pepper (at will). After 2 – 3 minutes, add the soy sauce, stir well. Add hot chicken broth (or hot water). Cook the dish over low heat for 30 minutes or until the meat softens. Add the buckwheat groats, put a lid on, let the dish simmer a low heat for another 4 - 5 minutes. Season it with salt, black pepper to taste. Remove the lid after 10 minutes.

Serve the dish warm, sprinkle with parsley.

68. Turkey Meatballs, Buckwheat, and Vegetables

Servings: 4

Ingredients:

- 1 lb (450 g) Turkey, mince, 7% fat

- ½ cup uncooked buckwheat groats

- 1 medium zucchini

- 1 small sweet onion, finely chopped

- 1 clove garlic, pressed

- 1 egg

- 3 tablespoons sunflower oil

- 3 - 4 tablespoons breadcrumbs

- **Spices:** 2 tablespoons finely chopped dill, 1 tablespoon finely chopped parsley, sea salt to taste, ground black pepper to taste

Instructions:

Rinse the buckwheat and put it in a saucepan with 1.5-cups cold water. Bring to a boil. Cook it about 3 - 4 minutes after boiling point. Then drain, set aside, for it to cool.

Meanwhile, grate the zucchini, sprinkle with salt. After 30 minutes, drain the water that has separated.

Mix the minced turkey, boiled buckwheat, zucchini, onion, garlic, egg, and all spices; stir well. Shape meatballs from the mixture with your hands and flatten them carefully. The number of meatballs depends on their size.

Preheat oven to 375 F / 190 C.

Roll the meatballs in breadcrumbs. Place them on a baking sheet sprayed with non-stick spray or oil. Sprinkle the meatballs with oil. Bake 15 minutes, then turn them and bake for an additional 10 – 15 minutes.

Serve with your favorite sauce or fresh salad.

69. White Fish Fillets with Buckwheat Sauce

(gluten-free recipe)

Servings: 4

Ingredients:

- 18.5 oz (520 g) fresh white fish fillets, cut into chunks

- 1 cup uncooked buckwheat groats

- 2 green onions, finely chopped

- 2 sticks celery, finely chopped

- 3 sweet mini peppers, finely chopped

- 1 tablespoon capers

- 2 tablespoons olive oil

- 3 tablespoons flaked almonds

- 4 lemon wedges

- **Spices:** 1 -2 bay leaf, 10 peppercorns, ½ teaspoon Italian herbs seasoning, ground black pepper to taste, salt to taste.

Instructions:

Rinse buckwheat under cold water. In a saucepan, combine the buckwheat with 2.5 cups of water. Bring to a boil. Reduce the heat to low and simmer 3 - 4 minutes. Set aside.

In a deep pan, heat the olive oil over medium heat. Add the celery, onions, and peppers, stew for 3 minutes, turning it occasionally. Then add herbs, capers, and buckwheat, gently stir.

Pour the fish over 2 - 3 cups of cold water, bay leaf, 10 peppercorns, and salt to taste. Bring to a boil. Cook the fish 10 minutes. Then remove with a slotted spoon.

Add 3 tablespoons of broth in which the fish has been boiled to the mixture with buckwheat. Season to taste with salt and pepper, gently stir.

On each serving plate, put 1/4 of the buckwheat mixture; on top of it, a portion of fish.

Garnish with almonds and lemon wedges.

70. Kale and Peeled King Prawns Buckwheat Pilaf (gluten-free recipe)

Servings: 4

Ingredients:

- 14 oz (400 g) cooked and peeled king prawns

- 1 cup uncooked buckwheat groats

- 1 handful kale

- Juice of ½ lemon

- 2 cloves of garlic, finely chopped

- 1 small onion, finely chopped

- 2 tablespoons olive oil

- 2 tablespoons sliced green olives

- **Spices***:* 1 tablespoon finely chopped dill, a pinch of ground black pepper, sea salt to taste, 4 lemon wedges

Instructions:

Rinse the buckwheat groats. In a saucepan, combine the buckwheat groats with 3 cups of water. Bring to a boil, reduce the heat, and let simmer until all the water is absorbed. This should take less than 4 minutes. Set aside.

Heat the olive oil in a saucepan. Add onion and garlic, saute 1 – 2 minutes. Then add the peeled king prawns, kale, green olives, salt to taste, black pepper, and lemon juice. Mix well. Once the kale has wilted, add the cooked buckwheat to the saucepan and heat through for a minute or so. Sprinkle with fresh dill. Serve buckwheat pilaf until it is warm. Garnish with lemon wedges.

71. Salmon Buckwheat Patties

(gluten-free recipe)

Servings: 4

Ingredients:

- 16 oz (450 g) fresh Atlantic salmon fillets

- ½ cup uncooked buckwheat groats

- 1 egg

- 2 green onion, finely chopped

- 1 – 2 pickled cucumber, finely chopped

- 1 small fresh carrot, grated

- 2 tablespoons olive oil or vegetable oil

- **Spices:** grated zest of 1 lime, 1 – 2 teaspoons Worcestershire sauce, 1 tablespoon finely chopped dill, a pinch of ground black pepper, sea salt to taste, zest of 1 lime

Instructions:

Rinse the buckwheat groats with cold water in a

colander, drain. In a saucepan, combine the buckwheat groats with 1.5-cup water. Bring to a boil, reduce the heat, and let simmer until all the water is absorbed. This should take less than 3 - 4 minutes. Set aside until cold.

Remove the skin of the fish with a sharp knife. Cut the salmon into chunks and place them in the food processor for a few seconds. Transfer to a deep bowl. Add egg, buckwheat, onion, carrot, pickled cucumber, and all spices. Mix well. Shape with oiled hands into round patties.

Heat oil in a large skillet over medium heat. Tilt skillet to coat the bottom of skillet entirely with oil. Cook the patties in the skillet until cooked through and lightly browned, about 5 – 7 minutes per side.

Desserts Recipes

R. Lazarova

This page intentionally left blank

72. Buckwheat Dark Chocolate Brownie

(gluten-free recipe)

Servings: 8 – 10. The number depends on their size

Ingredients:

- ¾ cup buckwheat flour

- 3.5 oz (100 g) Dark chocolate 70% cocoa

- 2.5 oz (70 g) butter

- 2/3 cup brown sugar

- 2 tablespoon cocoa powder

- ½ teaspoon baking powder

- 2 eggs

- ¼ cup warm whole milk

- ½ cup ground walnuts

- 2 tablespoons cocoa nibs (optional) or chocolate chips

- A pinch of salt

- Vanilla extract

Instructions:

Preheat the oven to 320 F / 160 C.

Grease a baking tray with a little butter, place baking paper on the bottom, and set aside.

Place chocolate and butter in the top of double over simmering water. Stir frequently with a rubber spatula until chocolate is melted, about 4 – 5 minutes. Set it aside and cool slightly.

In another mixing bowl, beat the eggs until fluffy. Add the sugar and mix well. Add this mixture slowly to the melted chocolate.

Sift together the cocoa powder, buckwheat flour, salt, and baking powder. Add the walnuts and cocoa nibs. Add together with vanilla extract to chocolate mixture, continually stirring to mix well. Pour the chocolate batter into the baking tray and smooth out the top.

Bake chocolate brownie in the oven until top is dry and edges have started to pull away from the sides of the tray, for 20 – 25 minutes. Once baked, leave to cool to room temperature. Cut it into squares. The number depends on their size.

73. Buckwheat Tart with Coconut Oil

(vegan recipe)

Servings: 1 Tart

Ingredients:

For this tart, you can use various fruits: apples, plums, figs, pears, and others. I made my apple tart.

- **crust:** 3 oz (85 g) organic coconut oil, 3.5 oz (100 g) buckwheat flour, 3.5 oz (100 g) whole wheat flour, 2 oz (55 g) brown sugar, a pinch of salt, vanilla

- **filling:** 1 lb (450 g) apples, a pinch of cinnamon powder, 1 tablespoon grated lemon zest, 1 - 2 teaspoons brown sugar, 3 - 4 tablespoons ground almonds or walnuts

- Tart Pan Removable Bottom

Instructions:

In a deep bowl, combine coconut oil, sugar, and vanilla. Add the whole-wheat flour, buckwheat flour, and salt. Mix the ingredients with either hands or a food processor to create a smooth, thick crust. Evenly distribute the mixture over the base of the tart pan, press firmly, and continuing 1.5 cm up the sides. Place in the fridge to set (10 – 15 minutes) until preheating the oven to 355 F / 180 C. Then put the tart pan in the oven, bake for 10 minutes.

Meanwhile, prepare the filling. Peel the apples cut them into two halves. Remove the seeds and cut them into thin pieces. Sprinkle with cinnamon, lemon zest, and sugar, mix carefully. Set aside.

Remove the tart pan from the oven. Sprinkle the tart base with walnuts (almonds). Arrange the apple slices on top in overlapping concentric circles. Bake the tart in the centre of the oven for 40 – 50 minutes. Once baked, leave to cool to room temperature. Cut it into thin pieces (8 – 12) and serve. The number depends on their size.

74. Easy Raw Buckwheat Crunch Balls

(vegan recipe)

Servings: the number depends on their size

Ingredients:

- ½ cup uncooked buckwheat groats

- ½ cup oat flakes

- 10 - 12 dates

- 4 – 5 dried figs, finely chopped

- 1.5 oz (40 g) golden seedless raisins

- ½ cup ground walnuts

- 1 tablespoon sesame tahini

- ¼ teaspoon vanilla

- 3 - 4 tablespoons coconut flakes

Instructions:

Rinse buckwheat with cold water. In a saucepan, combine the buckwheat groats with 1.5 cups of cold water.

Cover with a lid. Bring to a boil, reduce the heat, and let simmer until all the water is absorbed. This should take less than 3 – 4 minutes. Set aside until cold.

In a bowl, pour the oat flakes with ½-cup hot water. Set aside until cold.

Remove the pits from the dates. Pour over with 1/3 cup hot water for 15 - 20 minutes. Then place them in a food processor or strong mixer until it forms a smooth paste.

Combine buckwheat, oat flakes, dates paste, figs, raisins, walnuts, sesame tahini, and vanilla in a large deep bowl. Well knead the mixture with your hands. Form small balls that roll into the coconut flakes.

75. Buckwheat Pumpkin Dessert

(vegan, gluten-free recipe)

Servings: 4

Ingredients:

- ½ cup uncooked buckwheat groats

- 3 cups baked or boiled pumpkin (or can 15 oz / 425 g pumpkin puree)

- 1 tablespoon honey

- 1/3 tablespoon ginger, grated

- A pinch of cinnamon powder

- ½ cup walnuts, ground

Instructions:

Rinse buckwheat with cold water. In a saucepan, combine the buckwheat groats with 1.5 cups of cold water. Cover with a lid. Bring to a boil, reduce the heat, and let simmer until all the water is absorbed. This should take less than 3 - 4 minutes. Set aside until cold.

Place baked pumpkin in a food processor or strong

mixer until it forms a smooth paste. Transfer it to the large bowl. Add buckwheat, ginger, cinnamon, honey, and 2 tablespoons walnuts. Stir well.

Serve out the mixture into bowls. Sprinkle each serving with walnuts.

76. Quick & Easy Buckwheat Berries Dessert

(vegan, gluten-free recipe)

Servings: 4

Ingredients:

- 1 cup uncooked buckwheat

- 1 cup fresh or frozen berry mix blueberries, raspberries, blackberries, strawberries

- 1 small apple, cut into pieces

- 2 tablespoons almonds, ground

- 1 tablespoon maple syrup

- vanilla to taste

- 4 tablespoons grated dark chocolate for sprinkling

Instructions:

Rinse buckwheat with cold water. Put it in a deep bowl and pour it with hot water to cover it. Set aside a few hours and best all night. Then remove the water and put it in a food processor. Add the nuts and fruit. Turn on the processor for a few seconds until it forms a smooth paste. Add maple syrup and vanilla; stir well.

Serve out the mixture into bowls. Sprinkle each serving with grated chocolate. Put the dessert in the fridge. Serve after 30 minutes.

Bread Recipes

This page intentionally left blank

77. Buckwheat Bread with Coconut Milk

(vegan recipe)

Servings: 1 bread

Ingredients:

1 cup = 125 grams.

- 1 ½ cup buckwheat flour
- ½ cup whole-wheat flour
- 2/3 cup coconut milk
- 3 tablespoons olive oil
- ½ teaspoon baking soda (vegan)

1 ½ tspns baking powder.
(Rule : 3 x baking soda)
or bicarb.

-
- a pinch sea salt

Instructions:

Preheat the oven to 355 F / 180 C.

In a deep bowl, mix buckwheat flour, whole-wheat flour, baking soda, and salt.

In a mixing bowl, stir together the coconut milk and olive oil. Add the flour and stir well. Set aside a couple of minutes to thicken. Place the batter into the Pan – bread and smooth out the top. Cut 3 – 4 slashes on top with a bread knife. Bake for 25 – 30 minutes. Then remove the bread from the oven. Place it on a baking rack, cover with a kitchen towel, and set aside for 30 minutes.

78. Buckwheat & Chickpea Bread

Servings: 1 bread

Ingredients:

- 1 cup buckwheat flour

- 1 cup chickpea flour

- 2 cups whole-wheat flour

- 1 cup white bread flour

- 0.25 oz (7 g) dry yeast

- 1 – 2 teaspoons brown sugar

- 1 teaspoon of sea salt

- 1.5 cup of warm water

Instructions:

In a deep bowl, mix all dry ingredients. Add the warm water gradually, stirring constantly, knead a soft dough. Place it in a deep bowl, cover with a kitchen towel. Let rise in a warm spot until it doubles in volume (about 60 - 80 minutes). Then transfer the dough in a pan – bread. Cut 3 – 4 slashes on top with a bread knife. Again, cover with a kitchen towel and leave warm for 40–50 minutes.

Preheat the oven to 390 F / 200 C. Bake the bread for 30 minutes. Then remove it from the oven. Place it on a cooling rack, cover with a kitchen towel, and set aside for 30 minutes.

79. Buckwheat and Whole-wheat Bread

Servings: 1 bread

Ingredients:

- 1 cup buckwheat flour

- 3 cups whole-wheat flour

- ½ cup Oats (processed into oat flour)

- 5 tablespoons Oat bran

- 0.25 oz (7 g) dry yeast

- 1 – 2 teaspoons brown sugar

- 1 teaspoon of sea salt

- 5 tablespoons of milk powder

- 1.5 cup of warm water

Instructions:

Combine in mixing bowl all ingredients (without the water). Then add water, knead by food processor approximately 3 – 4 minutes until soft dough. Form it into a ball. Cover with a kitchen towel. Let rise 50 – 60 minutes in a warm spot. Shape dough into a loaf and place in a pan-bread with parchment paper. Cover with a towel set aside 40 minutes.

Preheat the oven to 390 F / 200 C. Bake the bread 30 – 35 minutes. Remove pan-bread from the oven, remove bread from pan, and place on a cooling rack. Cover with a towel. Serve after 30 minutes.

80. Buckwheat Buns

Servings: 4 buns

Ingredients:

- ½ cup buckwheat flour

- 1 cup bread flour and ½ cup for kneading

- 1 tablespoon Flaxseed + 3 tablespoons warm water

- 1 ¼ teaspoon active dry yeast

- 1 – 2 teaspoons brown sugar

- ½ teaspoon of sea salt

- 1 tablespoon sunflower oil

- 0.5 cup of warm water

- Sesame seeds for sprinkling

Instructions:

In a small bowl, put the flaxseed and pour it with warm water. In another bowl, stir yeast and sugar into warm water. Set both aside.

Stir remaining ingredients together; then add flaxseed and the yeast. Mix the dough until it forms a ball. Remove dough from bowl and knead a few times until the dough becomes slightly elastic. Depending on how sticky the dough is, you may need to knead in the extra flour. Place the dough in an oiled bowl. Cover with a towel and set in a warm place to rise for about an hour. After an hour, punch down dough and form into rolls. This makes about four rolls. Let rise for another 30 – 40 minutes. After the rolls have risen, brush lightly with water, then sprinkle with sesame seeds. Bake for about 20 minutes at 390 F / 200 C.

Remove buns from the oven, and place on a cooling rack. Let cool slightly; then slice in half to make burger-ready buns

Printed in Great Britain
by Amazon

78369260R00106